BABYTEETH

Rita Kalnejais

CURRENCY PRESS
SYDNEY

belvoir

CURRENCY PLAYS

First published in 2012
by Currency Press Pty Ltd,
PO Box 2287, Strawberry Hills, NSW, 2012, Australia
enquiries@currency.com.au
www.currency.com.au
in association with
Belvoir, Sydney.

Reprinted 2021, 2024.

National Library of Australia CIP data is available from the National Library of Australia Catalogue: http://catalogue.nla.gov.au

Typeset by Dean Nottle for Currency Press.

Cover design by Tim Kliendienst, Alphabet Studio.

Contents

For Chris Wheeler—my very dear friend—thank you.

Babyteeth was first produced by Belvoir at Belvoir St Theatre, Sydney, on 15 February 2012, with the following cast:

TOBY	Kathryn Beck
ANNA	Helen Buday
THUONG	David Carreon / Sean Chu
GIDON	Russell Dykstra
MOSES	Eamon Farren
HENRY	Greg Stone
MILLA	Sara West

Director, Eamon Flack
Set Designer, Robert Cousins
Costume Designer, Alice Babidge
Lighting Designer, Niklas Pajanti
Composer, Alan John
Sound Designer, Steve Francis
Assistant Director, Kit Brookman
Fight Choreographer, Scott Witt
Stage Manager, Luke McGettigan
Assistant Stage Manager, Liz Astey

CHARACTERS

HENRY
ANNA, his wife
MILLA, 14, their daughter
MOSES, 25
THUONG, 7
GIDON, music teacher
TOBY, Henry's daughter

PLAYWRIGHT'S NOTE

The occasional unconventional use of punctuation and grammar in this script is intentional, especially the non-use and misuse of commas. Characters use commas like they use air. Often these people are breathless—a breath at that moment would change the course of history. Changes of topic mid-sentence without pause for breath or semi-colon indicate that schism between what is being said and where the actual attention is placed. The spaces between sounds and between thoughts are almost always more important than the words themselves.

Outbursts in upper case are where the violence of feeling is like possession.

A forward slash indicates the point where the next speaker interrupts.

The 'what the dead said moments' in bold type are questions of production. They can be spoken outright or communicated as a change in the air through light, sound, a child's handwriting, snow, dogs—anything that communicates the miracle of sudden presence. Note: voice-over must not be used unless it's brilliantly, brilliantly, brilliantly subliminally embedded. Whatever the form, it must be a lovesong.

This play went to press before the end of rehearsals and may differ from the play as performed.

PART ONE

1.

THE MORNING AFTER THEIR LAST NIGHT ON EARTH.

The kitchen. It is morning. HENRY *sits at the table.* ANNA, *standing, rolls her shoulders, listens to herself breathe as if preparing for a boxing match.*

ANNA: I could make pancakes.

HENRY: I don't think I've got time for um… I can't keep re-/ scheduling.

ANNA: / Okay. We don't want a suicide on our hands.

HENRY: I'll be back at three.

ANNA: The appointment's at three.

HENRY: I'll be back at two. Fifteen. Two thirty. Two/ twenty.

ANNA: / We can get a cab if it's/ going to be difficult.

HENRY: / Two fifteen. I'll be back. I'll be back.

ANNA: You never have time for pancakes.

HENRY: Anna, my first client's/ at nine thirty. Peak hour—

ANNA: / Do you even like my pancakes, Henry?

HENRY: I don't really like pancakes full stop. I never have.

ANNA: Have you heard anything?

> HENRY *pours himself a bowl of cereal.*

[*Quietly, gesturing with her head towards the closed door*] It's very quiet. Don't you think? [*Raising her voice conversationally*] Don't you think, Henry… Have you really never liked my pancakes?

HENRY: I don't mind them. They're just always such a big/ deal.

ANNA: / I don't make them as punishment. I mean they're not exactly a walk in the park for me.

HENRY: I just think it's a waste of resources. If you're going to use eggs I'd rather have soldiers.

> ANNA *squeezes his hand.*

ANNA: You've got milk on your glasses sweetheart.

> *He wipes them clean.* ANNA *looks towards the closed door.*

Do you like that cereal?

HENRY: It's fine.

ANNA: It's different./ God, I can't stop eating—

HENRY: / Is it?

ANNA: You got the wrong one.

HENRY: / Did I?

ANNA: / —But it's really only you who eats it, so… Have I been getting one you're nonplussed about all this/ time?

HENRY: / No. No, I liked the other one. They're very similar… This one, I guess it's got more/ nuts.

ANNA: / More nuts! You like nuts.

HENRY: Within reason. There's peanuts.

ANNA: Well, I guess you can pick them out—

HENRY: They're not really a/ breakfast nut.

ANNA: / —rather than letting it ruin your day d'you think they're having sex?

HENRY: Yes.

> ANNA *bangs her head on a surface to hand.*

Gently.

ANNA: / What?

HENRY: / Be gentle. Don't concuss yourself.

ANNA: Have you heard something?

HENRY: No, but you know what young people are like.

ANNA: I'm scared I'll hear something.

HENRY: Well, just keep talking then.

ANNA: She'd be quiet but I don't know. He'd— I'm pretty sure he'd make a point of… We'd hear him.

> HENRY *eats. She picks up the box of cereal.*

Breathing or something. [*Reading the back of the box*] This one has a lot of hidden benefits.

> *She studies it closely. Taking a deep breath.*

> *Another breath.* HENRY *gives her a warning look. He reaches out to touch her hand. She stands quickly.*

[*Voiceless*] Don't I'll [cry]— Don't. [*Conversationally*] I can't stop eating. It's making me feel so sick but I just can't stop. [*She exhales, folds some hair behind her ear.*] How's Florence Bazzano? Is that right? Is she the one who can't stop sniff/ ing her fingers?

HENRY: / That was so wrong of me to tell you about/ her—

ANNA: / Who would I tell? Honestly? Who am I going to/ tell?

HENRY: / I shouldn't talk about clients Anna.

ANNA: I'm not asking for her address and shoe size. Henry. I'm genuinely interested in whether she's still sniffing her fingers and pretending she's/ not.

HENRY: / No—

ANNA: / Good.

HENRY: / —And thank you for showing such concern for my patient's well/ being.

ANNA: / Good. You're welcome. So the electroconvulsive/ therapy works well for sniffing because—

She sniffs.

HENRY: That's not why we treated her with electro— It was the only symptom I told you about. I thought you'd like it… I thought it would cheer you/ up.

ANNA: / Oh.

She leans on the sink. She fills a glass with water.

Can you knock on the door and give her this?

HENRY: Anna, they're probably post-coital…

She knocks her head again.

Gently.

ANNA: Come oooooon. She needs to start lining her stomach by nine or the whole day gets thrown out.

HENRY: It's only just past/ eight—

ANNA *tries to forcibly wrap his fingers around the glass.*

ANNA: / Just give the door a little tap Henry—

The door opens. MOSES *emerges. He is twenty-five, thin, tousled hair with one side flat from sleeping on it. His arms and fingers are covered with home-cut tattoos. He pulls on jeans as he enters.*

Good morning sleepyhead! Henry milk on your glasses. That was a good long sleep. Is Milla awake?

MOSES *shakes his head.*

I didn't hear her in the night. Did she sleep/ through?

MOSES: / Um. No. No. She woke up 'bout I don't know two?

HENRY *and* ANNA *look at him expectantly.*

She went to the toilet.

Pause.

HENRY: Are you/ hungry?

ANNA: / D'you want pancakes!?

MOSES *shrugs a yes.*

[*To* HENRY] They're not a punishment for everyone.

MOSES *goes to the stove and lights a cigarette on the burner. He sits at the table.*

D'you mind smoking outside Moses? We're a/ non-smoking house.

MOSES: / Sorry.

He stands, accidentally knocking his chair over, and stands smoking in the doorway. No-one rights the chair.

ANNA: But she slept through? Apart from that. She didn't need her/ morphine. [*To* HENRY] That's great huh?

MOSES: / Yeah, pretty much.

ANNA: That's great. That's her first night without it in about… five weeks?

She smiles very warmly at MOSES.

MOSES: She—

ANNA: It's great.

MOSES *nods. Coughs.*

I'll get onto the pancakes. Henry hates my pancakes I dis/ cover this morning.

HENRY: / I don't hate them. I'm/ ambivalent.

ANNA: / He thinks soldiers would be a better use of— Shall I make a tray to take in? To have in bed?

MOSES: I might—

HENRY: Give him a break Anna.

MOSES: … might take a/ shower.

HENRY: / He needs a break.

ANNA: I just thought they could/ eat together—

HENRY: / Sit down, Moses.

ANNA: —she needs to wake up and/ eat something anyway in a moment—

MOSES: [*to* HENRY, *raising his cigarette*] / I'll just finish.

> ANNA *goes to the fridge.*

ANNA: Well, we're out of eggs. Is toast okay?

> *She puts two heels of bread into the toaster.*

MOSES: She said when she woke up. To go to the toilet. The room was full of people.

ANNA: Oh.

MOSES: They said she said they were saying she could.

ANNA: What?

MOSES: They were saying she could stop struggling.

> ANNA *knocks over the milk. It spills on the floor and pools.*

ANNA: I didn't hear her get up. I do usually. With the light... I see her walk past our door and call out just to/ check.

MOSES: / She didn't want the light on.

ANNA: Do you have to go Henry?

HENRY: In a moment.

ANNA: They said she didn't have to struggle—

MOSES: She could/ stop.

ANNA: / This was a dream?

HENRY: Don't read too much into it, sweetheart. Our subconscious offers up all sorts of ways of coping with/ pain.

ANNA: / Did she say who they were?

MOSES: She said she remembered one of them.

ANNA: Really? Where/ from?

MOSES: / And there was some kid—

> *The toast jumps up.* ANNA *starts.*

ANNA: A kid.

HENRY: [*standing*] So... Vege/ mite okay?

MOSES: / Um, I might just have muesli if that's/ okay.

HENRY: / Of course it is. [*He gets a bowl from the cupboard.*] Sit down.

> *He puts a hand on* MOSES'*shoulder. He picks up the carton of milk.*

Oh, we don't have milk. [*To* ANNA] Do we? Have more milk?

ANNA: / No.

MOSES: / That's okay. I don't have it with milk usually.
HENRY: Ha. Lucky.

ANNA, *ominously silent, fills a glass with water, gets a cracker from the pantry and shakes two different pills into her hand.*

[*To* ANNA] Not like that/ sweetheart—
ANNA: / What?
HENRY: Don't wake her like that.
ANNA: I—
HENRY: Come here.

He stands up and takes her by the wrists. She breathes deeply. She notices he isn't wearing trousers and bursts out laughing.

ANNA: Are you not going to wear pants today?

She loses control, and on that moment that could become laughter or tears, shudders into a sob.

[*To* MOSES] I find it so funny that idea of going to see a psychiatrist and he's forgotten. It'd be like a bad dream and you'd think it was your problem. And you wouldn't say anything—

She frees her wrists and moves towards the bedroom.

HENRY: Anna.

MOSES *stands.*

ANNA: I'm laughing! What? It's funny. You'd go in to talk about how screwed up you were and then.../ it's so wrong.
HENRY: / Anna. Calm down first.
ANNA: I'm just laughing. It's okay to wake someone when you're... I'm laughing.

She stands with her hand on the doorknob. She looks to MOSES.

MOSES: It's pretty funny.
HENRY: Just give it a moment.
ANNA: Fine.

She crosses the kitchen and exits into the garden.

HENRY: Ten breaths.
ANNA: [*offstage, getting faster till she's hyperventilating*] One two three four fivesixseven joking I'm joking. Henry.

HENRY *and* MOSES *eat in silence.*

HENRY: Do you need anything?

> MOSES *shrugs.*

Show me your hands. Hold them out.

> MOSES *holds out his hands. They are shaking.*

Here.

MOSES: / Wh—?
HENRY: / Just valium.
MOSES: Should give her one.
HENRY: Don't take them all at—

> MOSES *throws them all back at once. He doesn't pause from eating.*
> *Struggles to swallow. He coughs drily like a cat.*

I know I can trust you to give Milla her medication because I know until very recently you worked as a dealer, so I trust—I trust you understand the importance of the correct dose, Moses. [*He stands to get* MOSES *a glass of water.*] You know how dangerous medication can be—

> ANNA *comes back inside and, face to face with* HENRY *again,*
> *bursts out laughing.*

ANNA: I can't stop thinking about the pants and just— [*hardly comprehensible through her laughing*] —going in because... you've been brutally... and you're saying trust issues trust issues and Henry's all mmmhmm mmmhmm right and/ the—
MOSES: / What?
HENRY: I can't understand her.
ANNA: —sorry. I just can't stop [*managing a breath*] eating. It's so weird. I just ate her cracker as well. I just...

> *She gets some more crackers. Starts to cry again as she eats.*

[*As she goes outside again*] I hate these [crackers—] [*Offstage*] Deep breaths deep breaths.
HENRY: [*to* MOSES] You need anything else?

> MOSES *shrugs.*

I'll bring you back some methadone when I get back at two. Fifteen. Do you/ want me to [do that—?]
MOSES: / Yeah.

HENRY: [*nodding*] Okay then. [*He leans back.*] I assume you've just had sex with my daughter. I'm right in assuming that? Thank you. Thank you. I know that neither of you would feel the need for protection. She's young and I know that… condoms are the last thing on anyone's mind. I won't do you the disservice of estimating how many STDs you've picked up over the last however many years. Please try to understand though that Milla has no resistance. If she contracts any secondary infections— Do you understand? She'd die of herpes. I don't think she'd die of crabs but/ it would be so [uncomfortable—]

MOSES: / I don't have crabs.

HENRY: Yes, I think we all would have been scratching if that were the case sorry that was a joke— I know as well that some of Milla's medication will be affecting certain natural… secretions. [*Without looking at* MOSES, HENRY *places a tube of lubricant and several condoms on the table.*] I don't want you to hurt her. I realise we both have complicated feelings about this conversation. I'm only too, too acutely aware of the bloodbath this would culminate in if we were Greek, I don't know you might be Greek Moses again that's a joke obviously I'm very uncomfortable.

ANNA *enters.*

MOSES: I'm not Greek.

ANNA *smiles magnanimously at* MOSES *and* HENRY *as she moves towards the bedroom door.* MOSES *stands.*

HENRY: [*dropping his voice*] But please understand that—

MOSES *moves towards the back doorway, his eyes following* ANNA. *He takes out another cigarette.*

I know how much you mean to her and I'm grateful.

ANNA: [*knocking gently as she opens the door*] Sweetheart… sweetheart…

HENRY: Please don't hurt her any more than you have to— I know it means nothing—

A sharp intake of breath from ANNA. MOSES *lights another cigarette on the stovetop.*

HENRY: —coming from me Moses but I'm begging you, I'm—

ANNA *enters. She stares at* MOSES.

ANNA: She's still warm.

> HENRY *leaps up, knocking his chair over. He rushes to the bedroom.*

She's still warm.

MOSES: She was dead already.

ANNA: You come in/ HERE YOU—

MOSES: / I woke up and she was already dead. She looked peace/ ful—

ANNA: / NOT NOW SHE DOESN'T SHE DOESN'T LOOK SO PEACEFUL NOW WITH HER EYES ROLLED BACK LIKE THAT

MOSES: I closed/ them.

ANNA: / THEY OPENED! WHY DIDN'T YOU CALL ME? WHY DIDN'T YOU TELL ME? WE COULD HAVE RESUSCITATED HER MAYBE SHE'D STILL… MAYBE… maybe— We didn't say goodbye

MOSES: She was dead, she was already dead.

ANNA: STOP SMOKING IN MY HOUSE, YOU… FUCK!

> *She hits his chest.*

I DIDN'T SAY GOODBYE. SHE DIDN'T SAY GOODBYE TO ME.

> MOSES *stops protecting himself.* ANNA *beats and beats his chest.*

YOU COME HERE AND YOU SMOKE US OUT AND YOU COME HERE AND YOU USE HER UP YOU'RE THE ONE WITH THE LAST WORDS WHO GETS TO HOLD HER HAND WHO GETS TO HOLD HER AND YOU USE IT ALL UP

> HENRY *comes in.* ANNA *keeps beating at* MOSES. HENRY *sits.*

HENRY: Anna. He's not responsible. Anna. Anna,/ Anna.

MOSES: / Sorry. Sorry.

> *When she has exhausted herself,* ANNA *drops her arms. Her knees buckle.* MOSES *tries to catch her.*

I'm sorry

> *He tries to help her up.* ANNA, *without looking at him, fights him off.* HENRY *wearily moves* MOSES *to the side and helps* ANNA *stand.* ANNA *walks slowly outside.*

I'm sorry. Anna.

> HENRY *puts his hand on* MOSES *'shoulder.* MOSES *'body shudders.*

2.

WHEN MILLA MET MOSES ON PLATFORM 19, CENTRAL STATION, 3.46 P.M.

The 3.44 train departs.

A crowd of greased-up, slick-back'd pigeons fling themselves at the sky. Feather and lice fall on the platform with their shadows.

RECORDED ANNOUNCEMENT: The next train on platform 19 is due in five minutes. This train will go to Lidcombe, stopping at all stations and then direct to Berala. And then to Regent's Park.
  Please stand clear of the yellow line and allow passengers to alight before boarding. Please stand clear of the yellow line.

> MILLA, *fourteen, school uniform, stands very close to the yellow line looking up at the timetable. Absently rolls her skirt at the waist with one hand.*

> *She turns to face the tracks. Her breathing is shallow and fast. She presses a violin case to her chest.*

> MOSES, *twenty-five, stoned, sits on a bench beside* THUONG, *seven.* THUONG *plays a handheld Nintendo and wears headphones. He listens to music.* MOSES *nods to the side, his head dropping onto* THUONG, *who shrugs him off, never taking his eyes or hands off his game.*

> MILLA *looks up through the smashed glass ceiling of the station, at the squall of pigeons, doomed skywriting plane, clouds, unbelievable space.*

> BRETT, *a station attendant, is forced to take the microphone, yellow sweat moons under his armpits.*

BRETT: Stand clear of the yellow line. Can the girl in the maroon uniform please stand clear of the yellow… stand clear of the yellow line or we'll be required to send someone down.

MOSES: Hey. Hey/ hey hey hey

BRETT: / Can the girl in the maroon uniform stand clear of the yellow/ line.

MOSES: / hey!

MILLA *turns around.*

Are you the girl in the/ maroon uniform?
BRETT: / Can the girl in the maroon uniform—

MILLA *looks up.*

Yes, you, move away from the yellow line.
MOSES: [*pointing to the line*] Yeah it's just…

MILLA *jumps back.*

BRETT: Thank you. Next time you'll be arrested.

MOSES *fists the air in the direction of the nearest speaker.*

MILLA: Thanks.

She sits on the bench beside him.

MOSES: [*gesturing to the violin case*] What's that?
MILLA: Ruger. M77 Hawkeye.
MOSES: Cool.

MILLA *looks away.*

They wouldn't press charges. They wouldn't press charges 'cause
you're underage so fuck 'em y'know. Fuck.
MILLA: Oh. With the/ yellow—
MOSES: / Fuck 'em.
MILLA: Yeah.
MOSES: [*gesturing*] You ever taken anyone out? With your…/ Ruger—
MILLA: / It's a violin.

MOSES *looks at her blankly.* MILLA *flashes the case open at him.*
THUONG *snaps a look into the case.*

MOSES: Yeah I sort of [knew that]… You any good?

MILLA *shakes her head, closing the case.*

I bet/ you—
MILLA: [*shaking her head*] / No—
What?
MOSES: Your hair's like—
MILLA: What?

She folds a piece behind her left ear.

MOSES: It's like bangles.

MILLA: Bangles.

MOSES: When you shake it… bangles. With the light. 'Cause it's…/ Bangles.

MILLA: / Thank you.

>MOSES *shrugs.* MILLA *looks down.*

[*After a moment, very politely*] Yours is nice too.

MOSES: Yeah, but look at that. Cut myself.

>*He bows his head to show her.*

I had to go on a weird angle to get to that bit. You see? And the clippers sort of/ slipped.

MILLA: / You did it yourself? You cut your own/ hair?

MOSES: / 'Eah.

>MILLA *looks at him intensely.* MOSES *runs his hand over his head self-consciously.*

What?

MILLA: Looks good.

>MOSES *runs his hand over his head again.*

MOSES: Can't stop touching it. You want to feel it?

>MILLA *puts her hands on his head. After a moment she folds her hands in her lap.*

Um.

MILLA: What?

MOSES: You got um—There's/ blood—

MILLA: / Oh— [*Her nose is bleeding.*] / It's okay.

MOSES: / Shit. [*To* THUONG] You got a tissue?

>THUONG, *squeamish, continues playing his computer game.*

MILLA: It's fine. It's just a/ blood [nose].

MOSES: [*to* THUONG]/ Come on man…/ Shit—

MILLA: / It's fine

MOSES: It's getting on/ your skirt.

MILLA: / It doesn't matter. It happens all the/ time… Oh…

>MOSES *starts taking his shirt off.*

MOSES: / Here—

MILLA: It's just my nose… don't—

He holds it out to her.

Oh, no. No. Thanks./ No.

MOSES: / Come on. Don't want to get it on your top.

He raises it to her face.

MILLA: No. It's/ okay—
MOSES: / Lean back.

She lets him raise it to her face.

Lean back. I've got ya. Find a bit of sky. Just stay back. Nah—

He cradles her head with his hand. She leans her head back without conviction.

You got some/ sky?

MILLA: / Can you take it off my face—it just really [smells]— Sorry. [*Sitting up, coughing*] It's gone down my/ throat—
MOSES: / You right? Spit? Okay—

She spits. It runs down her chin.

MILLA: Sorry.

She spits again. Her hair is mussed. She tries to smooth it. MOSES *wipes her chin with his t-shirt.*

MOSES: We'll just/ wipe [that]—
MILLA: / I can [do it]— Thanks.
MOSES: [*smoothing back the hair that has come loose*] Okay.

He leans her back again.

MILLA: Is there blood in my hair?
MOSES: Yeah. Bit.

After a moment:

MILLA: I always wear it in this stupid pony. I never wore it down. It's the longest my hair's ever been and it looks so nice out. I don't know why I never wore it down.

She lets her head relax into his hand for a moment.

MOSES: Holy shit!
MILLA: What?
MOSES: That tooth is so little.

MILLA *closes her mouth. She starts coming up.*

You/ right—
MILLA: / Fine. I think it's fine now. [*She spits.*] Thanks.
MOSES: Where you going?
MILLA: [*indicating her violin case*] Lesson. Where are you going?
MOSES: Visit a friend.

She looks at his shirt.

MILLA: There's so much blood—

MOSES *shrugs. She gives the shirt back to him.*

MOSES: Sort of saved your life, hey?

MILLA *smiles with her mouth closed.*

Hey—

MILLA *cleans up her face.*

MILLA: Is my face clean? Is there any/ blood left?—
MOSES: / Little bit of—

He leans in to clean her face. MILLA *is very still.*

MILLA: Where?

MOSES *rubs some blood from her chin.* MILLA *breathes quickly and quietly.*

MOSES: You're right. Hey—
MILLA: / Thanks.
MOSES: / I hate to ask you this… it's just… I've been thrown out of my house—
MILLA: / evicted?
MOSES: / 'eah. And I'm sort of trying to put some money together to get a bed in a shelter for the night. If you get there late you sort of miss out/ and—
MILLA: / Why d'you get evicted?
MOSES: Oh… like I got a bit behind on my rent 'cause I've got this… I get quite bad eczema and my medication's like really expensive so— Look, I hate to ask you hey you just seem like a really nice person/ and—
MILLA: / How much?
MOSES: Just whatever you can manage. Sorry to ask hey.

She studies him intensely.

It doesn't have to be much just 'cause I saved your life or whatever—

She opens her violin case.

I'd be really grateful hey.

MILLA *takes out a pale blue envelope. Looks inside.*

Just whatever you can/ manage.

MILLA: / I'll give you fifty if you/ do something for me.

MOSES: Fifty! That's too much. I don't/ want to—

MILLA: / Twenty then.

MOSES: No fifty's okay. I just don't want to put you out. Like I'm really sorry. It's just like it's been really hard lately and like—it's just been really hard but/ fifty'd be great.

RECORDED ANNOUNCEMENT: / The next train to arrive on platform 19 will be stopping at all stations to Lidcombe and then direct to Berala. And then to Regent's Park. Please stand clear of the yellow line and allow departing passengers to alight before boarding. Please stand clear of the yellow line. This train…

THUONG *stands.* MOSES *stands. He scruffs* THUONG'*s hair.* THUONG *shrugs him off with sudden force.* MILLA *looks up.*

MILLA: Oh.

MOSES *looks up.*

Look at that… cloud like a… I don't know.

MOSES *looks to the train.*

MOSES: We gonna take this one?

RECORDED ANNOUNCEMENT: Stand clear of the closing doors please.

He reaches out his hand to her.

MOSES: We'll miss it.

MILLA: Just a cloud./ Isn't it?

/ *The doors of the train are closing.*

But very white.

WHAT THE DEAD SAID TO MILLA: PART 1.

They said: Take his hand.

The train departs. MILLA *and* MOSES *are left alone behind the yellow line. The platform dissolves into some kind of sky.*

MILLA *looks up.*

MILLA: I guess it could be a dragon. Or.

> She takes MOSES' *hand.*

I keep coming back to the fact it looks like a cloud.

Then they said: hold on.

ANNA AND HENRY KEEP THEIR TUESDAY APPOINTMENT.

Henry's office. HENRY *eats the second half of a sandwich.* ANNA *lies on his professional couch, looking out the window.*

ANNA: I told him I wanted to move towards a classic bob and/ then—
HENRY: / It does look like you're moving towards a classic/ bob.
ANNA: / I don't think you understand the terminology Henry. I don't want him to touch my hair at all really but he's closing an hour early to give Milla some privacy. So I said just do my roots at the same time so it's worth your while. So I guess I'll be sitting under the heat while/ Milla's—
HENRY: / There's red onion in/ this.
ANNA: / Is there?
HENRY: I can take it out.
ANNA: I feel he sort of guilted me into it.
HENRY: He guilted you into it?
ANNA: I mean I suggested it but he would have, you know? How he… how he… you know— And Milla said she didn't want me just sitting fussing when she was being done so I'd just be waiting in the car otherwise. And I know I'd run in at the last minute and say just do anything and walk away with layers or a—

> HENRY *glances at his watch.*

Is my time up?
HENRY: Not quite.
ANNA: I'm just boring you. What time is it?
HENRY: Quarter past.

> HENRY *eats.*

ANNA: Quarter past… Henry.

> *She flashes her knickers at him.*

HENRY: Really?

ANNA: I think so. Don't you?

HENRY looks at his watch.

You/ don't.

HENRY: / No, I'm/ always—

He looks at his watch again.

ANNA: When's your next client?

HENRY: She's due at four thirty. I'm just thinking, though… she's always at least/ ten minutes—

ANNA: / Let's just do it. Don't you reckon?

HENRY looks at his watch again.

Denise will buzz, won't she? [*Taking off her knickers*] Come on. It's the last thing we'll feel like next Tuesday.

HENRY chews very fast, his eyes glazed with concentration.

Chew your sandwich properly. We're okay. Aren't we?

HENRY: While I remember…

He gets a small bottle of pills from inside his desk. He throws it to her. She doesn't catch it. She finds the bottle, takes a pill immediately and puts it into her bag. He holds his sandwich out to her.

ANNA: With/ food?

HENRY: / Mmmm.

She takes a bite of his sandwich. She gets up.

ANNA: I see what you mean about the red onion. [*She hangs her knickers on the lamp on the desk.*] Bit of atmo/ sphere—

HENRY: / Make sure you take those before you [go]—

He chews fast. He reaches out to touch the small of ANNA's back and slides his hand down. He pats her arse. Tries to swallow.

She picks up a picture on HENRY's desk. She narrows her eyes at it.

Where are your glasses?

ANNA: When was that taken? I don't/ know where I put them.

HENRY: / August 0-10?

ANNA: 0-10 August… She looks like a kid, doesn't she?

HENRY: She's just gotten the all clear there. That was that drive to Austin/ mer—

ANNA: / Oh… it's that beer garden overlooking the water. I see… That's why she looks like that.

HENRY: What?

ANNA: Didn't you sit on fifty all the way there and all the way/ back?

HENRY: / I didn't at all. Did she say/ that?

ANNA: / I'm just playing Henry. She said it was great.

HENRY: I love that photo. That light's just/ stunning.

ANNA: / But she looks so pissed off.

HENRY: That's just—no she's just squinting because she's looking into the sun.

ANNA: Why do you always make her do that?

HENRY: That's how you get that beautiful… look at that sky. That's *National Geographic* standard sky.

> ANNA *puts the photo down.*

ANNA: How are you going with that sandwich?

HENRY: A couple of clients have said it looks like a professional portrait.

ANNA: But they're crazy Henry. Is it kosher to have these showing?

HENRY: If I think a client's going to get fixated or over-involved I clear the/ desk of [any personal]—

> ANNA *is suddenly impatient.*

ANNA: / Come on.

HENRY: You were/ asking—

ANNA: [*glancing at the couch*]/ D'you want to use a towel?

HENRY: I think I left it at the gym. I can't/ find it.

ANNA: / Okay. Clear the desk then.

HENRY: That's not what I meant when I said—

> HENRY *methodically lays the objects from the desk onto the floor while* ANNA *undoes her blouse.*

ANNA: How's the gym going?

HENRY: It's okay. I've got a bit more [*demonstrating*] range of motion in the left [leg].

> *He places the clock on the floor so it faces him.*

ANNA: Is Seamus pleased with you?

HENRY: [*her bra*] This is nice.

ANNA: [*reaching behind to unclasp it*] You say that now but… this… is the bra that gives you the foul mouth.

> HENRY *reaches around to snap open her bra.*

HENRY: I don't think Seamus cares actually. He's pleased he's— Oh God. I remember this—/ Shit. Shit.

ANNA: / Wait a sec— Here.

> *They swing the bra around so the clasp is at the front. They both work with enormous focus at unclasping it.*

HENRY: Shit. Bloody hell. Shit.

ANNA: I'll just leave it on.

HENRY: No. I've done it—bugger—before, haven't I?

> ANNA *takes* HENRY*'s hand and places it over her breast. She kisses him. He is loathe to stop working on the clasp.*

Bugger.

ANNA: That's so good to kiss… red onion.

HENRY: I told them not/ to [put it on—]

ANNA: / Push your knee between my legs… Is that going to pull?

HENRY: I think that's okay—

ANNA: You o/ kay?

HENRY: / [Ow] Uh-huh.

ANNA: Henry—just leave that clasp. It's/ fine.

HENRY: / No no, I've remembered the trick. I've done it before—

> *The phone buzzes.* HENRY *reaches for it.*

[*Into the receiver*] Really? Give me… five…?

> *He snaps open the bra. Is delighted with himself.*

[*Into the receiver*] Three…

> *He puts his hand on her breast.*

[*Into the receiver*] If you could get her MRS scan ready that'd be great.

> ANNA *re-fastens her bra.*

[*Mouthing to* ANNA] What are you doing? [*Into the receiver, his hand on* ANNA*'s breast*] There's a more recent one than that.

ANNA *starts dressing.*

[*Into the receiver*] Third week of January, something like that?

> ANNA *puts on her underpants. She takes another of the pills* HENRY *has given her.*

[*To* ANNA] Sorry. Are you okay?

ANNA: See you tonight.

HENRY: Love/ you.

ANNA: / Love you.

> *She leaves.*

WHEN ANNA VISITED GIDON IN UNIT 48, FIFTH FLOOR, OVERLOOKING THE GARDEN BY THE BINS. SHE STOOD IN THE HALLWAY.

ANNA *stands in the hallway and knocks on the door of unit 48. Her skirt is tucked into the back of her underpants. Inside the unit someone is playing piano with their left hand. She listens at the door. Knocks again.*

GIDON: [*faintly from inside*] Ej elle… pis sudu. [Fuck off… fuck.]

> *The door is swung open by* GIDON—*his shirt plastered to his back hangs open, froth of sweat like a racing horse, glasses held together with a safety pin and bandaids. He looks her up and down.*

ANNA: Milla's mum. [*Pointing into the room*] Is she learning Paga/ nini?

GIDON: / You bring my bow?

ANNA: Sorry.

GIDON: My bow.

ANNA: Your bow?

GIDON: My bow.

ANNA: Your bow? No.

GIDON: Su'ds. [Shit.]

ANNA: Sorry I'm so late. I hit the school traffic on Wellington. And then that roawork on Christy anyway— The intercom thing downstairs seems to be broken.

> *He shrugs.* ANNA *glances at* GIDON*'s chest. His shirt hangs open.*

Is Mil/ la ready [to go]?

GIDON *follows* ANNA*'s eyes.*

GIDON: / Oh, my goodness. [*Doing up the bottom button with one hand*] Excuse me. Oh, my goodness. Excuse me/ please—

ANNA: / Can I—?

GIDON: Please.

He makes himself more comfortable, filling the door frame.

ANNA: Can I have her back?

GIDON: She does not coming.

ANNA: I'm/ sorry—

GIDON: / She does not coming.

ANNA: Mr Gi/ don—

GIDON: / Just Gidon. Is first name. Is/ *foreign.*

ANNA: / M— Gidon sorry Gidon I arranged to meet Milla here. Has she left?

GIDON: No listen: she does not coming today.

ANNA: No, I'm picking her up here. I'm meeting her/ here.

GIDON: / She leave a small message saying I am not coming.

ANNA: [*glancing down at his chest*] Is this the truth?

GIDON: You think I *lying*? All week I wait for today and then this fucking/ shit.

ANNA: / Did she sound upset? In the/ message?

GIDON: / More relieve maybe.

ANNA: I've planned this so badly. Sorry. I'm meant to be taking her to get her hair cut. Obviously she's going to be upset—

GIDON: Milla's mum… maybe—

ANNA: Sorry

GIDON: Maybe this haircut… is not so important.

ANNA: It is. Sorry, M[r]—Gidon./ Sorry—

She turns to go.

GIDON: / Milla's mum. Your [skirt]—

ANNA: I wasn't accusing/ you of lying.

GIDON: / Tell Milla she please must to bring back my bow.

ANNA: I really don't think she has your/ bow.

GIDON: / She is taking my bow last week.

ANNA: I'm sure it was an accident. If she does/ have your bow.

GIDON: / Yes, of course is accident. I'm sure is not to sell on the eBay.

ANNA: I'll make sure you get it./ If she has it.
GIDON: / Thank you, Milla's mum.
ANNA: Anna./ Sorry—
GIDON: / Anna, yes sorry. Anna. She definitely has.

>   ANNA *turns.*

> Anna—your/ skirt.
ANNA: / If she does I'm sure it's by/ accident—

>   GIDON *steps up close, reaching for her skirt.*

GIDON: / Your skirt—
ANNA: [*shooing him away aggressively*] What are you doing?!

>   THUONG, *backpack, headphones, head down, walks down the hall.*
>   *He has a key on a chain at his belt.*

GIDON: It is in/ the panties.
ANNA: / I've got it. [*Adjusting her skirt*] Sorry.

>   *Seeing* THUONG *disappearing…*

GIDON: [*to* THUONG] Hey! YOU! ASIA! HEY! [*To* ANNA] How old you
think is this boy?
ANNA: I've no idea. I'll make sure Milla returns the bow.
GIDON: Thank you, Anna.

>   ANNA *departs hurriedly, her hand smoothing the back of her skirt.*

> [*Calling after her*] Anna—is perfect now. No need for this. Is perfect.

>   *She rushes off.*

WHEN MILLA BROUGHT MOSES HOME TO MEET HER PARENTS, ANNA AND HENRY.

MILLA, *her hair freshly shaven into a soft mange of mohawk and rat's tails, a little dried blood around her nose, stands with* MOSES. MOSES *wears his bloody shirt. He scratches his arm and left waist.* HENRY *wears a short-sleeved shirt.*

HENRY: Moses./ I'm Henry.
MILLA: / and this is my dad Henry. And MUM! MUM!
MOSES: / Pleased to meet you Henry. Moses. Pleased to meet you.
HENRY: [*to* MILLA] She/ went to pick you up.

MILLA: /Shit./ Shit. I totally meant to call.

> / *The phone rings.* HENRY *and* MILLA *blink at each other.*

HENRY: [*answering*] She's/ here.

MILLA: / Sorry Mum. Sorry/ sorry

HENRY: No no. No. I think… No—just come home. You're almost here now/ so um—

> MOSES *runs his hand over her head and pulls his hands through the rat's tails, squealing quietly.* MILLA *giggles.*

MILLA: [*to* MOSES] I can't stop feeling it. It's so snakey.

HENRY: [*into the phone*] —ten breaths. You want me to count—okay. Okay. She's brought a friend home— [*Turning his body away to speak very quietly*] Maybe take one of the blue ones and two white ones. No, [*glancing at* MOSES] I think you can take the whole one. [*Back to his public phone voice*] You can cancel that. No no, cancel it. Get your roots done if you want but— Okay. See you in a moment. No, I think we're fine. But you have one if you want.

> *He hangs up.*

MILLA: / Whoops.

HENRY: / It's okay. She's just flustered. It's just she rushed to get there.

MILLA: I was on my way but then I ran into Moses and he does hair. And he sort of offered so… And I had a blood nose which is what happened last time I got it cut. So it was lucky I didn't have to go to the salon with those stupid/ work-experience girls… with stupid Grant—

HENRY: / Look, I think it's very sensible to have a friend do it. It's lucky you happened to run into/ each other—

MOSES: / Rats' noses bleed when you raise a scalpel to cut them.

> HENRY *takes a moment to take this in.*

HENRY: Well we all have very complex physiological responses to stress.

> MILLA *smiles proudly at* MOSES.

MILLA: D'you like my new haircut, Dad?

HENRY: Haircut?

MILLA: Henry.

HENRY: You look like you could rough me up.

He wrestles her.

MILLA: Dad!

He gets her into a soft headlock.

HENRY: Promise not to headbutt me!

MILLA: [*under his armpit*] Say you like it.

HENRY: Of course I— *Ow!* I love having a heavy as a daughter.

> MOSES*'mobile phone registers a message. He checks it. His face briefly hardens.*

[*Quietly into her newly exposed ear*] Did you take your Aristocort?

MILLA: Oops.

She breaks out of the headlock and runs out of the room.

HENRY: [*to* MOSES] Biblical…/ Moses.

MOSES: / 'eah.

HENRY: Can I get you a drink?

> MOSES *nods.*

[*Trying to ascertain his age*] A beeeeeeeeeeeeeeeer?

MOSES: Yeah

HENRY: She's not legal, you know.

MOSES: Sorry?

HENRY: Okay so a beer.

> ANNA *rushes in, flustered.*

ANNA: [*to* HENRY] You were there when we/ arranged it, weren't you?

HENRY: / Anna—

ANNA: I was always going to pick her up from/ violin—

HENRY: / This is Moses.

ANNA: Oh! Hi!

MOSES: Hi

ANNA: Moses bib/ lical.

HENRY: / Biblical I was just saying that.

He comes around and rubs her shoulders.

[*To* ANNA] How you going?

ANNA: Oh. O… kay.

HENRY: Good. No harm done. Just a change of plans.

ANNA: [*as if in code*] Ye-ah-s.

MILLA *enters.*

MILLA: Mum… sorry.

ANNA *is very, very still for a moment.*

ANNA: You've got some trimmings on your face.

She reaches out to brush them.

MILLA: Mum

ANNA: Look at this. [*Tentatively touching* MILLA*'s hair*] What's this called?/ Is this a style?

MOSES: / Rat's tail.

ANNA: [*really nodding*] It's/ a style?

MILLA: / Moses cut it for me. My nose was bleeding/ and he—

ANNA: / Your nose was/ bleeding—

MILLA: / Mum it's just a blood nose… He offered to do it for me. So…

ANNA *tries to brush* MILLA*'s face.*

ANNA: You're stressed. It's when she gets stressed. I/ knew it—

MILLA: / Don't.

ANNA: Grant closed the salon an hour early for us so it could be more/ private this time.

HENRY: / Moses pointed out that rats' noses bleed when they're about to be cut with a scalpel.

ANNA: I don't understand what that means. They're actually very pretty. The trimmings. They're like little Pele's hair… Henry aren't they? It's— 'Pele's hair' is when bits of larva from volcanoes— Is this right—in the South Pacific? Henry? Is this/ [right]?

HENRY: / Ha/ waii. Pele—Hawaii.

ANNA: / Hawaii. And it blows over the sea and collects in strands on branches of trees on… what?… nearby…/ what?

MILLA: / Great.

ANNA: [*to* HENRY] Have I/ said something…?

MILLA: / You hate it.

ANNA: Nnooooooooooooooooo. No—

MILLA: You/ do.

ANNA: / —it's good to play with it for a bit. I think it's really great. [*She rolls her shoulders and her neck, really enjoying her body right now. Turning to* MOSES] Are you a hairdresser?

MOSES: My mum used to breed bishons.

ANNA: [*very casually*] Aaaah. And that's how you know about rats, is it?

MOSES: That's why I've got clippers. They're poodle clippers but I use them on me as well.

ANNA: And you like those as your tools? You get a result you're happy with using the poodle clippers?

MOSES: They're just like regular clippers. Bit louder.

HENRY: And less accurate I can imagine.

MOSES: No. We were competitive. Mum was a three times state winner with her bishons.

ANNA: Was she? Henry? That's very impressive. [*She nods at* MILLA *in a 'What a catch' way.*] And so you two—

MILLA: Mum!

ANNA: What? [*To* HENRY] What? [*To* MILLA] How did you meet?/ Is that okay?

MILLA: / On the way to violin.

ANNA: Today?

MOSES: / 'eah.

MILLA: / No. Officially yes/ but—

ANNA: / And instincts told you he could be trusted to give you a bishon cut? How old are you, Moses?

MILLA: / Sevent[een]—Twenty. One. Five.

MOSES: / Twenty-five.

    HENRY *and* ANNA *nod, both actively not looking at each other.*

ANNA: Well. I'm a bit freaked out but lucky for everyone I forgot I'd already taken a Xanax when I took two Ativans and then god something blue… which probably is about to— [*rolling her left shoulder*] kick in… so I'm feeling verrrrrrry/ relaxed physically. I hope this isn't a stroke… Do I look relaxed? I can hardly keep the left side of my face up.

HENRY: / It's certainly very nice to meet a friend of Milla's from outside her immediate circle. Of friends.

    ANNA *starts giggling*

ANNA: Sorry. Henry. [*To* MILLA] It's so obvious your dad's/ freaking out.

HENRY: / How many did you take?

ANNA: What you said to take. But I took that Xanax before I went to pick her up. And two Ativans and then what you… the ones you just… on the— [*She drops her phone and scrabbles to pick it up.*] Sorry, Mil. Oh, is that a bit scratchy?

MILLA: I've just… no… I've/ got some hair down my back.

ANNA: / Have a shower. Cool you down.

MILLA: You have a shower.

ANNA: I ju-u-u-ust might. Do   that. What's in that bag?

MOSES: Figs

> ANNA *takes them and looks in the bag at length.*

ANNA: This isn't going to work.

MOSES: Can you put them on a windowsill or something so they/ ripen?

> / *She chromes the bag.*

ANNA: That smells so green. That is really what green smells like.

HENRY: It's not dangerous. She's just very relaxed.

ANNA: [*to* MOSES] Lucky for you. Now, Moses, you've got a drink. Because you're TWENTY-FIVE!!!! Why not? Where did these come from?

MOSES: We picked them from next door.

MILLA: They looked like light bulbs. I couldn't reach so Moses/ got them for me.

MOSES: / The fucking honeyeaters get them if you leave them too long.

MILLA: I couldn't reach them—

HENRY: Mmm.

> HENRY *hands* ANNA *a glass of water with ice cubes.*

ANNA: [*to* MILLA] You look like a different person. [*To* HENRY]/ Doesn't she?

MILLA: / Good.

HENRY: Your cheekbones look very fine. You actually look more like Anna now.

> MILLA *throws her hand to her forehead. It lands heavily.*

ANNA: Ow. She's got a great shaped head for it. We got a big happy surprise last time, didn't we, when we shaved it. We were nervous, I was I was nervous. [*To* MOSES] She was verrrrrry overdue. And had that what d'you call them, um… [*She gestures. To* MOSES] What's that word?

MOSES: A vase?

HENRY: Inden/ tations.

ANNA: / Indentations!—for *months* after. She had to be induced but then they used the forceps and she started to pull them up inside me because she just didn't want to come out. But we got her. And here we all are.

HENRY: / Moses what do you do? You're not a hairdresser.

ANNA: / That's why there's no baby pictures up because her head was so indented. But/ now... [*gesturing each side of her head filling out*] it's fine. She's so beautiful.

MILLA: / Is that true? Henry—

ANNA: And that's why I can't look at peanuts. I was/ ripped to shreds but that's—

MILLA: / Oh, my/ God.

HENRY: / Anna, do you need a lie down or a walk around the block?

ANNA: I'm sorry, Milla. I'm so high. [*Leaning in to* MOSES] You know she'll lose that ratty thing? It's very painful.

HENRY: Anna.

MILLA: It's not actually. Not at all.

ANNA: Not painful like that.

MOSES: You've got blood in your mouth.

ANNA: What?

MOSES: Your mouth is bleeding.

>   ANNA *spits blood.*

ANNA: [*very casually*] Sorry. [*To* MILLA, *not at all sorry*] Sorry, I was chewing my ice.

HENRY: That tooth.

ANNA: I've had a loose tooth. It's not a baby tooth. Only Milla has/ baby teeth.

MILLA: / That's an aberration. It's an aberration for someone as old as me to have a baby tooth.

MOSES: Which one is it?

MILLA: / This one—

ANNA: / I have been neglecting my dental hygiene and—

>   MILLA *turns her face to* MOSES. *He takes her face in his hand.*

MOSES: [*peering*] That little guy... It's so small—ha!

ANNA: —I'm only sorry that it's to come to a head in front of your new twenty-five-year-old friend.

MILLA: Mum. Can't you feel you're/ drooling?

HENRY: / Sorry Moses.

ANNA: Don't apologise to him. For me.

> MOSES *takes out a cigarette.*

Not around Milla.

MILLA: Mum!

ANNA: Go outside.

> MILLA *looks to* HENRY. MOSES *moves towards the back door.* MILLA *cuts him off and presses against his shoulder. She presses against him with the whole of her body.*

[*To* MOSES] I think someone should ask you to leave.

> ANNA *looks at* HENRY *and slowly, slowly, as if each frame were broken down, raises her cuff to her mouth to wipe it.*

MOSES: [*to* MILLA] D'you have that… um…?

MILLA: Oh, yeah. Sorry. Sorry. Yeah—

> *She opens her violin case, takes out the pale blue envelope.* MOSES *tucks it into the back of his jeans.* ANNA *covers her mouth. She looks away.* HENRY *puts his hand on her.*

ANNA: Moses.

> *She passes him the bag of figs.*

> *He gives the bag back to her as he leaves. She runs to the window to watch him walk away. She lays the figs along the windowsill.*

3.

WHEN IT WAS DIFFICULT NOT TO TAKE THE ROTATION OF THE EARTH PERSONALLY. WE ALL JUST DID WHAT WE COULD.

It is morning. ANNA, *standing, rolls her shoulders, listens to herself breathe as if preparing for a boxing match. The radio is on, slightly off station. Outside in the far distance a dog barks.* ANNA *fills a glass with water, gets out a cracker and gently goes into Milla's room.*

The dialogue in the bedroom is barely audible.

ANNA: [*offstage*] Good morning.

> MILLA *stirs in her sheets.*

MILLA: [*offstage, just woken*] Don't.

ANNA: [*offstage*] I/ know.
MILLA: [*offstage*] / Ow.
ANNA: [*offstage*] Good girl.
MILLA: [*offstage*] Mum…
ANNA: [*offstage*] Can you manage a little bit of water, d'you/ think?
MILLA: [*offstage*] / Can we get a bishon?
ANNA: [*offstage*] A bishon! Oh. We'll have to— Good/ girl. We'll have
to think about that…

> TOBY *walks by the kitchen window, heavily pregnant and carrying
> boxes.*

TOBY: / *Henry!*
ANNA: [*offstage*] D'you want the curtains open a little/ bit?
MILLA: [*offstage*] / No—
ANNA: [*offstage*] It looks like a lovely/ day.
MILLA: [*offstage*] / Don't—Mum!
TOBY: *Henry!* Come here!

> HENRY *trots into the kitchen. He peers out the window.* ANNA
> *comes back into the kitchen.*

HENRY: [*kissing* ANNA *on the cheek*] Unsettling—

> *He takes the sleep from her eyes with his finger.*

ANNA: Oh. Yuck. Thanks—
HENRY: [*glancing towards Milla's room*]/ Is she awake?
ANNA: Just. Throwing up until six.

> *With one hand she turns down his collar.* HENRY *goes into Milla's
> bedroom.*

HENRY: [*in the doorway*] Big night…?

> *In the kitchen* ANNA *places each fig from the windowsill in the ray
> of light thrown by the morning sun.*

MILLA: [*offstage*] Can we get a bishon, Dad?
HENRY: [*offstage*] Oh. What does Mum/ say?
MILLA: [*offstage*] / Um yes?
ANNA: What was/ that?
MILLA: [*offstage*] / Yes…?

> ANNA *smiles to herself in the kitchen.*

HENRY: [*for* ANNA*'s benefit as well*] Well, bishons all round then if Mum says/ yes—

ANNA: / I didn't— [*louder*] yet

MILLA: I'm/ serious, Dad.

TOBY: / *Henry!*

ANNA: [*under her breath*] God.

TOBY: [*offstage*] *Come ON Henry you fucking/ mongrel—*

HENRY *re-enters the kitchen. He looks out the window.*

HENRY: / It is. It's very [*tuning the radio*] unsettling. That keeps slipping, doesn't it. Have I missed the news... [*looking at his watch*] mmmm—

MILLA *enters.*

ANNA: Good morning!

She wears a nightie. Her skin is ashen. ANNA *helps her sit at the table. She gives her several tablets.* MILLA *orders them and takes one at a time.*

TOBY: HEEEEEEEENNNNNNNNRRRY! Come here! Come on, boy!/ Come on!

MILLA: / Go on, Dad!

HENRY: You've got to admit that's pretty unsettling.

MILLA: W/ [whoa]—

HENRY: / Are you going to throw up?

MILLA *pushes her medication away. She gets up shakily and gets her violin.* ANNA *puts a glass of water by the tablets.*

MILLA: [*to* ANNA] I'll take them in a bit.

ANNA: Good girl.

She sits back at the table. She plays several notes of a scale. ANNA *hums a C, trying to tune* MILLA. *She hums it again.* ANNA *turns off the radio. She hums it again.*

MILLA: Okay, Mum.

ANNA: It's just a bit/ flat.

TOBY: [*offstage*] / HENRY! COME OOON!!! YOU FUCKING FUCKING/ MONGREL FUCK—

ANNA: We're going to have to move.

MILLA: When I lift my arm there's like—

She drops the violin. ANNA *gasps and reaches out impulsively.*

It's sort of pulling—

ANNA: Can you feel anything there like a—a lump or—?

MILLA: It's the port.

ANNA: [*to* HENRY] We should get that checked/ out— [*To* MILLA] Could I just have a feel—?

MILLA: / It's just the port. Don't—

ANNA: Can Dad have a little/ look?

HENRY: [*to* ANNA] / Just mention it to Ruth when you go in.

ANNA *puts the violin back on the table.*

ANNA: Is it just the pulling feeling or is there a swelling?

MILLA: I don't know.

MILLA *picks up the violin again and lays her chin in the rest.*

ANNA: Maybe there's something they can do so it doesn't… pull like that. If it is the port— [*Turning to* HENRY] Is there? Maybe put the… valve in another… direction or something to free up that action a/ bit—

/ MILLA *drops the violin onto the ground.*

Milla! Be/ careful!

HENRY: / Whoops! It's okay. Everyone's just a bit/ … tired.

ANNA: / It's a very expensive violin!

MILLA *takes one of her pills.*

We'll work out a way so it doesn't hurt. I know it's… We'll work out a way so you can still play. It's okay. It's not da/ maged—

MILLA *pushes it to the ground again.*

GO TO YOUR ROOM! YOU GO TO YOUR ROOM NOW UNTIL YOU LEARN RESPECT!

HENRY: She doesn't have to—/ Milla—!

MILLA *gets up.* HENRY *stands to help her.*

MILLA: / 'S okay, Dad.

MILLA *goes into her room.*

ANNA: Sorry—

MILLA *slams her door.* ANNA *knocks gently.*

Milla? Sorry. Sweetheart. Sorry.

MILLA: [*offstage*] Fuck off.

ANNA: Okay. [*Quietly*] We have to find a way so it doesn't hurt her. I bet there's a really/ simple way—

HENRY: / Give it a rest today/ Anna.

ANNA: [*quietly*]/ Violin is so important to her, Henry. You can see how upset this makes her—

HENRY: She can't lift her arm.

MILLA: [*offstage*] YES I CAN!

ANNA: We're not talking to you!

> HENRY *winces. So does* ANNA.

Sorry. [*Calling out*] Sorry Mill. [*Quietly to* HENRY] She's got a lesson this afternoon, what should I/ do?

HENRY: / Cancel.

ANNA: But… she loves it Henry./ She's just—

MILLA: [*offstage*] / I DON'T LOVE IT!

ANNA: YES YOU DO. Sorry sorry— [*To* HENRY] Do you have to/ go yes—

HENRY: / I'll just…

> ANNA *gives him the medication from the table.*

ANNA: Can you—make sure she takes these.

> *He goes into Milla's bedroom for a moment. A moment later he closes the door.*

> ANNA *picks up the bow. Looks at it carefully. Turns the radio on louder and louder. She moves the figs further into the ray of light which has slipped with the city turning quietly to face the sun.*

> HENRY *comes out of the bedroom. He squeezes* ANNA's *shoulder as he leaves. She smiles at him with her mouth closed. She rolls a still-green fig against her lips.*

HENRY MEETS TOBY AND CHANGES A BULB.

TOBY *walks past* HENRY *carrying two boxes stacked on top of each other. She smiles as she passes. He smiles back a little awkwardly.*

TOBY: Shit. Got a little… Shit… Can you/ help me—?

HENRY: / You right?

TOBY: Take this take this—jesus fucking—fuck. Oh shit.

She almost throws the boxes to him and puts out the starter spark of a small potentially horrific fire incident on her shirt.

Bit of ash. This dress is so flammable. Imagine if I went up in flames—

HENRY: You shouldn't be smoking.

TOBY: I know. I need both hands.

HENRY: You're pregnant—you shouldn't be smoking. You shouldn't be smoking/ anyway.

TOBY: / They've done a study. No, I know that's popular but they've done a study and it's okay actually. [*She smiles.*] It's science. They did a bit of a science, you know…? As long as you don't smoke tailor-mades in the last trimester it's okay—

HENRY: That's rubbish.

TOBY: No it's not—it's online—and no camembert. No soft cheeses. It's a study. Actually. It's the chemicals. HENRY!!!!

She takes the boxes off him.

But it is dangerous smoking and carrying boxes in a viscose dress. That's dangerous. If I'd been eating camembert at the same time it would've been completely irresponsible.

HENRY: You right with those?

TOBY: Look, I'm glad you thought I was pregnant. I think some people think I'm just morbid. You know? Fat? You know?

HENRY: You're obviously pregnant.

TOBY: Really?

HENRY: You're tiny. It would be a very bad sign if you weren't pregnant with a belly like that.

TOBY: You live there?

HENRY: Yes.

TOBY *nods, thinks, nods.*

TOBY: Did the woman here before me die?

HENRY: I don't know actually. I didn't ever meet her. I think Anna—

TOBY: Annayour…?

HENRY: My wife. My wife… she met her—

TOBY: Mmmm. Have you been married long?

HENRY: Twenty-three years.

TOBY: Whoa. I'm twenty-three. That must mean something. Um…

HENRY: Okay.

He starts leaving.

TOBY: HENRY! [*To* HENRY] I don't know where he is. He's a little cunt. I hope he hasn't been hit by anything. He was growling at the air... like I thought maybe the woman who used to live there was dead and he was in communication with her, you know?

HENRY: I have to get to work. You okay now with those?

TOBY: No I'm fine. Fine. Fine. Hey. Um... Can you stand on a stool for me? These blown bulbs. These bulbs have blown and I'll have to change them. Would you mind?

> HENRY *looks at his watch.*

It'll only take a moment. I promise I promise. I'm just so clumsy. I can't trust myself within five metres of a stool at the moment. [*She smiles at* HENRY *disarmingly.*] I never could really.

> *She ushers* HENRY *inside.*

ANNA *LEAVES THE HOUSE CARRYING GIDON'S BOW.*

She hesitates at the door for a moment, checks the back of her skirt.

HENRY AND TOBY. IN WHICH HENRY CHANGES A GLOBE, IS ELECTROCUTED, BANGS HIS HEAD, CONTINUES TO SPEAK COHERENTLY.

TOBY *shows* HENRY *a naked globe.*

TOBY: Thank you so much. It won't take a moment. So here's the stool... Thank you. I'll hold it. Is that okay? Oops. Is that okay? And here's... the new bulb. It's one of those energy saver ones. Is that off or on?

> HENRY *is buzzed.*

OH!!!!

> HENRY *falls backwards.* TOBY *screams.*

OH, MY GOD!

> *She gives* HENRY *a hand up. He electric shocks her. She screams.*

I'm sorry. I'm so sorry. Your head. I'm so sorry. I'm so sorry.

HENRY: I'm okay.

TOBY: Look at you. Look at you. I didn't... It's these old houses. Some of the electronics are crazy. Sit down. Oh.

HENRY: I'm okay.

TOBY: You can't be. I just electrocuted you. And then you hit your head. Sit. SIT! SIT! Good. Good… Just *stay*.

HENRY: It was just a little—

He searches for the word as if they were in his hands. TOBY *gasps.*

—shock. A little shock. It's—

He tests his pulse. Plants both feet firmly on the ground.

TOBY: I hope you're not brain damaged. D'you want a glass of water? Are you allowed around water? What's that rule with hairdryers? Ow… [*She puts her hand on her stomach. Softly, to her belly*] I know it gave you a shock. I know it did. Oooh, feel this…

HENRY: [*holding up his hands as if they were stun guns*] I'd better/ not.

TOBY: / Ha, yeah, you'd better [not]…

He sits on his hands. She sits on her hands with some difficulty.

Are you okay?

HENRY *nods.* TOBY *folds a bit of hair behind her ear.*

Just quiet. It's nice to just be quiet sometimes. Do you have kids?

HENRY *nods.* TOBY *nods.*

How old? My age? Not my age.

HENRY: She's fourteen.

TOBY: She's at school

HENRY: … Yes.

TOBY: Smart. Is she smart?

HENRY: She's good at Maths.

TOBY: Boring. Does she know what she wants to do? When she leaves school?

HENRY: Something with the violin maybe… [*He thinks hard. Taps his sternum.*] I'm not one hundred percent… sure…

TOBY: If she's good at Maths she can do anything. Anything boring… Are you okay?

HENRY: Yes.

TOBY: D'you think I'll be okay?

HENRY: How d'you mean?

TOBY: I'm just being stupid do you like Anex? As a boy's name?

MEANWHILE MILLA LEAVES THE HOUSE WEARING A CAP.

She bites her lip as she leaves.

HENRY AND TOBY CONTINUED.

HENRY: Anex?
TOBY: [*genuinely concerned*] Bit too much like Anus?
HENRY: Um./ No.
TOBY: / I don't want him to be teased. I guess I can't protect him from
   everything. Like—
HENRY: [*shaking his head*] Yes,/ n-no.
TOBY: / What names do you like? Oh, my God! I make you come in. I
   electrocute you. I don't know your name! I don't know your name.
   I'm Toby.

> *They shake hands. Electric shock.*

/ Ow.
HENRY: / Ow! Henry.

> *She looks at him blankly.*

Henry.
TOBY: Henry. You are *not*.
HENRY: I am. Henry Finlay. Henry Charles Finlay.

> TOBY *cracks up and hits him.*

TOBY: Henry's a dog's name! Henry! Sorry. Ow. Ow. All the dogs in my
   family have been called Henry. God, I hope he hasn't been run over.
   He's never been gone this long before. D'you think something's
   happened? He goes for these little jaunts but he always comes back.
HENRY: If he hasn't been run over or poisoned there's no reason he wouldn't
   come home this time. He's just exploring his new neighbourhood.
TOBY: Hopefully not being dragged around on someone's tyre, though.
   Hopefully that's not how he's seeing the/ neighbourhood.
HENRY: / I'm so sorry. I have to go. I've got a client—
TOBY: Of course. Of course you do. God. Um... d'you want me to wet
   down your hair? It's sticking up a bit.
HENRY: [*looking for a reflective surface*] Oh—

TOBY: No wait, I've got something that will be perfect. Wait. Don't move Henry. No fast movements or I'll— [*Doing a karate chop*] Ha! Sit! Ow.

> *She presents a tub of hair product.*

So… this is gel, but it smooths your hair.

HENRY: You'll be okay.

TOBY: Um—d'you want me to—? You put it on. Don't be shy of it. It dries very natural. Can I just…?

> *She styles it.*

No I won't do that. Oh… maybe…?

HENRY: How do I look?

TOBY: Not at *all* like a Henry.

HENRY: What do I look like?

TOBY: I don't know. I don't know. Someone from the future. Like…

> *She rests her hands on her stomach. He stands to leave.*

Henry.

WHEN MILLA WAITED ON PLATFORM 19, CENTRAL STATION: PART 2. IT DIDN'T FEEL LIKE A LOVE STORY THAT DAY. (IT WAS BUT IT DIDN'T FEEL LIKE IT.)

RECORDED ANNOUNCEMENT: The next train on platform 19 is due in one minute. The train will go to Strathfield, stopping all stations and then direct to Berala. First stop Redfern. Then Macdonaldtown, Newtown, Stanmore, Petersham, Lewisham, Summer Hill, Ashfield, Croydon, Burwood, Strathfield. Then express to Berala…

> MILLA *waits breathlessly.* THUONG *sits beside her. He wears head-phones and plays with his handheld Nintendo.* MILLA *looks up and down the platform. She starts to cry. She is careful with her eye-liner at first.*

This train will go to Strathfield, stopping all stations and then direct to Berala. First stop Redfern. Then Macdonaldtown…

Please stand clear of the yellow line and allow passengers to alight before boarding. Please stand clear of the yellow line.

> THUONG *stands.*

Stand clear of the closing doors please.

The train departs. MILLA *is alone on the platform. She blows her nose, and keeps waiting.*

WHEN ANNA VISITED GIDON IN UNIT 48, FIFTH FLOOR, OVERLOOKING THE GARDEN BY THE BINS. THIS TIME SHE CAME INSIDE.

ANNA *knocks at the door of unit 48. She smooths down the back of her skirt. She knocks again.*

GIDON: [*very quietly, from inside the apartment*] Hold your fucking horse—

> *The door is opened a crack and then flung open when he sees his bow.*

Anna! Anna! You bringing me my arm— Ohhhh! Is wonderful! Look at you! Beautiful!

> *He takes the bow from her hands. He places each hand on her face and kisses her.*

Come in! Come in!

> *He seizes her and dances her inside and around the room.*

Please sit— I bring you some—anything! Anything you like! Is yours! Say it!

ANNA: I c/ an't—

GIDON: / Say it!

ANNA: I can't stay, actually. I have to get back to Milla.

> GIDON *looks at her.*

GIDON: Where she is?

ANNA: She's not coming today. She wanted to but… [*She touches her hand to her heart where Milla's port sits.*] So I thought I'd better get your bow back anyway. No-one bid for it on eBay, so here it is.

GIDON: Anna, may I…? [*He gestures to the window.*] May I show you…?/ Please—

ANNA: / What?

GIDON: Something for you special. Down there. You see?

ANNA: The pigeons?

GIDON: No no, of course not. Why would I show you this pigeons?

ANNA: What am I looking for?

GIDON: See the blue flowers on that—

ANNA: No.

> *She slits her eyes, searching.*

GIDON: No, look closer… this bush by this yellow/ bin?

ANNA: / Nnn—

GIDON: Here.

> *He gives her his glasses. They are held together with a safety pin and bandaids.*

ANNA: Oh. Oh.

GIDON: I plant it four years since from a seed my brother send me, very illegal. This seed I drop in earth. I give her the shit and the blood and bone and now… Oh. You don't care—

ANNA: No I [do]— I'm sorry./ I just need to get home.

GIDON: [*loudly*] / You see. This blue flowers that are my memory of… first fucking when I am thirteen and, and with my, my brother wrestling behind the church—this flowers are growing out of the shit. And all the shit making this beautiful thing blue flowers. It is the nature romancing us. You see?

ANNA: They're lovely.

GIDON: I'm just saying, is all.

ANNA: No they're really lovely. Sorry.

GIDON: [*taking her hand*] Anna, tell me.

> *He leads her to the piano and clears the stool of manuscripts.*

ANNA: I've got some/ money for—

GIDON: You're shaking. Sit. Please please come. I make some space for you— Look is good place for you. Please.

ANNA: I need to get back.

GIDON: Please, Anna. Please.

> ANNA *sits at the piano, facing the keyboard.*

Thank you. Thank you. There's nowhere else to sit in this shitcunthole as you see. I'm so sorry. But is good for you, I think. You can face that way or or…

ANNA: Oh.

GIDON: … as you like. I get you some food.

ANNA: No.

GIDON: You/ need.

ANNA: / I'm really not/ hungry.
GIDON: / No sandwich?
ANNA: No/ thank you.
GIDON: / A coffee? Please.
ANNA: Okay. Just… but just a small one, I have to get/ home.
GIDON: / Thank you, a coffee. And a small slice of sausage.
ANNA: Okay. Thank you. That would be/ lovely.
GIDON: / Good!

> *He goes into the kitchen.* ANNA *spreads her fingers on the keyboard.* GIDON *enters, midway through, undoing his top buttons. He watches her for a moment.* ANNA *looks up and jumps.*

Milk?
ANNA: No.
GIDON: Sweetie.
ANNA: No.
GIDON: No sweetie?!

> ANNA *shakes her head.*

If you can play, you should play.
ANNA: Mmmm.
GIDON: You know this one?

> *He slams his fists on the keyboard.*

PIS SUDU! EJ DIRST DIEVS!!!

> *He goes into the kitchen.*

[*Offstage*] You know what is this song? Yes?
ANNA: No.
GIDON: [*offstage*] Is meaning 'Fuck You, God'! When God fucking you over and you so angry is shaking you from inside is a good song for you. And is Latvian so God can't understand what you saying. Is very convenient for me—

> *As he makes coffee* ANNA *looks at the keyboard.*

[*Offstage*] So Milla cannot come today. Is shame.
ANNA: Yes. She's so upset not to be able to…/ come—

> ANNA *looks at a framed soft-focus photograph of a woman in lingerie on top of the piano.*

GIDON [*offstage*] / Really?

ANNA: Is this your wife?

GIDON [*offstage*] What?

ANNA: This woman in the red… red G?

GIDON [*offstage*] / G…

ANNA: / bra… bra G-/ string.

GIDON: [*coming in with a tray*] No no. She is my brother's wife.

> *She takes a slice of sausage.*

Milla's mum, when will I see your daughter return? Please.

ANNA: I don't know. Actually.

> ANNA *starts coughing.*

GIDON: Will I see her again?

> ANNA *chokes painfully.*

No! You take the rind off. You don't eat the rind. It makes you choke like a cat, like a monkey.

> *He helps her cough.*

[*Holding out his hand*] Here. No, it's okay. You just spit into this. Never with the swallowing. No woman ever swallows around Gidon. Unless they insist.

> *They smile and nod as if he'd made a polite passing comment.*

ANNA: Sorry.

> *She spits into his hand.*

GIDON: No no, thank you. Thank you.

> *She starts coughing again.*

ANNA: Sorry… It's so gamey—

> *She stands and moves towards the door, laughing and coughing. Her eyes watering.* GIDON's *hand at her waist.*

I just need some air—

WHEN MILLA WAITED ON PLATFORM 19, CENTRAL STATION: PART 2 CONTINUED. IT DIDN'T FEEL LIKE A LOVE STORY THAT DAY. (IT WAS BUT IT DIDN'T FEEL LIKE IT.)

MILLA *sits alone on the platform. Her make-up is smudged from crying. She tries to fix it. She is too exhausted to leave.*

WHAT THE DEAD SAID TO MILLA: They said: Look up.

MILLA *looks up and sees a cloud.*

WHAT THE DEAD SAID TO MILLA: Then they said: This is the world. It is beautiful.

She takes a breath.

WHEN ANNA VISITED GIDON IN UNIT 48, FIFTH FLOOR, OVERLOOKING THE GARDEN BY THE BINS. THIS TIME SHE CAME INSIDE. CONTINUED.

GIDON *opens the door.* ANNA *takes a breath.* THUONG *passes.* GIDON *sees him and grabs him swiftly and unexpectedly.*

ANNA *screams.* THUONG *screams.*

GIDON: [*to* THUONG] Come—come here. I am not hurting you. Come here— Where your mother is?

 He lifts the headphones from THUONG*'s ears.*

[*Shaking him lightly*] What's wrong with your eyes? Look here. Look at me.

ANNA: What are you/ doing?

GIDON: [*lifting the headphones to his own ears*]/ What are you…? *Kuces dels!* [Son of a bitch!] What is this/ fuckshit?!

ANNA: / Stop it! Stop that! This is abuse! You can't do that to a child—

GIDON: / This—this is abuse. Is like Motherfucker, like—

 He flings the headphones across the room. THUONG *screams.*

—death in your ear— What's your name? He can't understand. Your/ name? *Ir mulkis*— [Is a halfwit—]

ANNA: [*to* THUONG] / I'm Anna. What's your name? This is Mr—

GIDON: / Just—

ANNA: / Gidon. I'm Anna.

GIDON: Tell her. Tell—Anna. Anna, we call him Roman, maybe is best.

 ANNA *looks at the name on his schoolbag.*

ANNA: Thuong. Is that right?

 THUONG *shrugs. He looks away.*

Thuong?

THUONG: Thuong.

GIDON: Thuong?! Thuong!?

>THUONG *looks away, irritably.*

Roman. [*Confidentially with* ANNA] Is best I think I go with this, Anna.

ANNA: Just listen—Thuong.

GIDON: Mmm.

ANNA: Your mum is home?

>THUONG *shakes his head.* GIDON *suddenly seizes* THUONG *again and carries him inside.* THUONG *kicks against him.*

GIDON: [*to* ANNA] All hours I see him with these shit on his ear. And coming home sometimes one, two in morning.

>THUONG *looks away.*

Give me your eyes. Who is looking/ after you?

ANNA: / Be careful! Be/ careful with him! Put him down.

>*She grabs him and places him on the ground.*

GIDON: / Where your mother is? He is not understanding what I'm saying. Look at his face.

>*He snaps his fingers in front of* THUONG'*s eyes.*

Look at these little arm. I get you some food.

>*He goes into the kitchen.* THUONG *makes a run for the door.*

[*Offstage*] Don't let him get away, Milla's mum. Or I break his neck.

ANNA: [*very quietly and quickly*] Okay, listen. The sausage is safe. It's very, very garlic-y but it won t hurt you. Don't eat the rind. Where's your mum? I'll call her or/ is there someone—

>GIDON *re-enters.*

GIDON: / Here we go— [*Forcing a piece of sausage into* THUONG'*s hand*] Here.

ANNA: You have to let him go home. [*To* THUONG] Don't!/ Don't touch the rind.

GIDON: Don't touch the rind!

>THUONG *watches them as they watch him eat.*

ANNA: You have to be careful with other people's children.

GIDON: Little fatty fingers. Good. [*He grabs the soft-focus picture from the top of the piano.*] Play with this while I get you—

ANNA: / Really?

GIDON: / What? She is dressed as elf. Look at him. He can't understand—

He fetches his violin and starts tuning it, listening intensely. He runs rosin along his bow.

[*Gesturing to the picture*] You see her waist? [*Showing the curve of the violin*] You see here? Anna, hold this… [*giving her the rosin*] rosin. Give me this.

He takes the picture from THUONG. *He very carefully and gently positions* THUONG*'s face on the chin rest. He places his hands in position.*

See. In your hands. You feel this? You feel this curve. And here on your chin. You see? You imagine it is the woman, you lie your face on her like this and… [*breathing out*] breathe with her… It's not like… [*He gestures towards the headphones.*] Not just in the head. It's in the feet [*slapping his toes*] and— [*his stomach*] It rise up through— [*stamping the ground*] and down through the sky to meet you [*his elbow and shoulder*] here. And it's like you are making love with. You see… you are making love.

ANNA: Is that/ appropriate—?

GIDON: / He cannot understand.

ANNA: [*to* THUONG] Do you speak English?

THUONG: Yeah.

THUONG *pulls out a few notes.*

GIDON: [*very gently, as if coaxing*] No no… Ow… No, is okay… Here we… Breathing, breathing.

ANNA is at a loss. She leans against the piano, pressing down several keys. GIDON *arranges* THUONG*'s fingers. And guiding his arm,* THUONG *pulls a very long, clear, perfect note.* GIDON *nods gravely.* ANNA *raises her closed hand to her chest as if her heart had been kindly broken by this one-noted ache of a song.*

ANNA RETURNED HOME AND MILLA WASN'T THERE. THIS IS WHEN SHE RETURNED.

ANNA *is in the kitchen. Everything inside her skin feels like ice.* MILLA *walks in. Her eyeliner is smudged down her face.*

ANNA: Where were you?

MILLA: I missed you.

> ANNA *seizes her in her arms.*

ANNA: I'm here. No. I'm here. I'm here. It's okay.

> ANNA *and* MILLA *hold onto each other very tightly.* MILLA*'s tears are very hot and very quiet and very salty.*

MILLA: Has my eyeliner run?

ANNA: It's okay.

MILLA: Can you fix me up?

> ANNA, *holding her tightly with one arm, uses her left hand to gently rub* MILLA*'s cheeks. The hand is clenched shut as she does it. She uses her knuckle the way she would on her own face.*

ANNA: Here we go.

MILLA: What are you doing?

ANNA: / What?

MILLA: / Open your hand, Mum.

> ANNA *opens her hand. Inside she holds the piece of rosin. She softly cleans around her eyes.* ANNA *holds* MILLA*'s face gently in her hand. And, cradling her close, supports her head in her hand as if she were a newborn baby.*

4.

ROUTINE: PART 2… 3 WEEKS LATER.

It is night. ANNA *stands in the kitchen. She rolls her shoulders as if preparing for a boxing match. She takes several pills from the fridge. Fills a glass with water and goes into Milla's room. She turns out the light as she goes. She is heard quietly talking to* MILLA *in the next room.*

LOOTING. IT WAS NIGHT TIME. MOSES BROKE IN LOOKING FOR A WAY OUT. MILLA FELL ASLEEP DREAMING OF A DIFFERENT BODY.

Night time. It is very dark. A faint flicker and buzz from a faulty streetlight. Distant clatter of dead stars.

The kitchen window smashes quietly. MOSES *slides his arm in and unlocks it. He jumps over the windowsill and balances for a moment on the edge of the sink. He knocks several figs to the floor as he jumps.*

ANNA, *appears breathless in the doorway and watches in the darkness.*

MOSES *starts rifling through drawers and cupboards. He finds boxes of prescription drugs.*

ANNA: [*quietly*] You ripping us off,/ Moses?

    / He starts, lets out a stifled, panicked scream.

    [*Closing the door*] Sssshhh/ ssshh.

MOSES: / I'll fucking kill you if you/ scream.

    He holds a knife out.

ANNA: / Just— Wait! Wait…

    She closes the connecting door.

MOSES: Don't/ fucking—

ANNA: [*pointing at the box in his hands*] / They're just going to make you throw up.

MOSES: Don't come any fucking closer.

ANNA: What are you gonna do, Moses? My husband's in the next room—

    MOSES *holds out his knife.* ANNA *steps back.*

MOSES: Get back from the fucking door. What… [*feeling his shirt*] what's that wet? Fuck—

    He glances towards the window.

ANNA: Is it money? Is it drugs?/ 'Cause I can—

MOSES: / If you come a step closer I will slice your mouth open, I swear to God—

ANNA: Please—

MOSES: What—?

ANNA: Don't. Don't—

MOSES: [*looking to the window again*] Fuck—

ANNA: I'll get you money I'll— [*She collects boxes of medication.*] These these will calm you down Moses./ These will um—

    Her hands shake as she goes around the kitchen.

MOSES: / Stop saying my fucking name—

ANNA: Sorry, um… There's codeine in that so…

MOSES: Why've you got so much/ shit here—

MILLA [*offstage*]/ Mum!

ANNA: [*very, very quiet—almost wordlessly*] Get out. Please. Don't hurt her.

MILLA [*offstage*] MUM! MUM!

ANNA: [*calling out*] Coming sweetheart.

>   *Silence.*

Get out.

>   MILLA *can be heard getting out of bed and falling.*

HENRY! HENRY!

>   MOSES, *panicked, holds his knife up. His reflexes are slow.*

MILLA: Mum!

ANNA: HENRY!

MOSES: Shut up—

>   ANNA *slaps the knife from his hands and pushes him towards the window.*

Fuck!

MILLA: Moses?

ANNA: It's just me sweetheart— DON'T COME IN HERE! I'm I'm just on/ the phone—

MILLA: / Mum? I/ heard—

>   MILLA *pushes the door open. She is dazed. Her head is completely bald.*

ANNA: / GO TO YOUR ROOM!! NOW!/ GO!!

MILLA: [*gasping*] / M-Moses?

>   *Her face lights up.*

MOSES: Milla

MILLA: You slipped—

>   HENRY *enters. He switches on the light. We see that* MOSES *has fresh bruises. That his arm is bloody from the break-in.*

MOSES: Milla

HENRY: What the/ hell? What the hell is going on here?

MILLA: / I thought I lost you. When you fell into the fig tree. It was funny at first. At/ first but—
HENRY: / What's he doing/ here?

> ANNA *looks towards the window.*

MOSES: / I w/ as—
MILLA: / I said come home—meet me at home— Your hand slipped Mo. I thought you were still holding my hand. I still can't feel that./

> *She bangs her hand hard on the table. Looks at it as if it were a fish flapping on a jetty.*

It's so loud in here—
ANNA: [*reaching for her*] / Darling we should/ get you back to bed—
HENRY: / I'm going to have to call the police/ Moses—
MILLA: / —sssssshhhh

> MOSES *takes* MILLA*'s fish hand. He holds it gently.*

Ooooooooh… it hurts. Does it? Is it hurting you/ No—
ANNA: [*trying to take her hand from* MOSES] / She's had something that makes her a bit/ woozy—
HENRY: [*to* MOSES] / That's a nasty/ cut
MILLA: / Those clouds'll cut you to shit seriously Henry. They look so comfy but you rub your face in them—
ANNA: / Come on sweetheart. Don't touch/ that. Don't let her touch that—

> HENRY *tries to forcibly take* MILLA.

MILLA: / Moses hold/ on DON'T—

> HENRY *pulls her away.*

—SLIP MO—MOSES—HOLD ONTO ME—HOLD ON **HOLD ON** HOLD ON HOLD ON
HENRY: / We might get you to leave now Moses. If you want to/ just—
ANNA: [*to* MILLA] / Sweetheart— It's okay. Come on—

> MILLA *reaches for* MOSES.

MILLA: [*seizing him*] I've got you you're/ okay it's okay
> *She holds him tight.*
MOSES: / Yeah. It's okay girl. You're okay./ You're okay

> MOSES *strokes her head.*

MILLA: [*quietly into his chest*] / We have to remember you're too hot for clouds

HENRY: Milla come on—

> MILLA *shakes her head.*

Come on— We/ can't just

ANNA: / Henry

> MILLA *sees* MOSES *'arm.*

MILLA: Ow. I can fix this.

> *Staying close to* MOSES, *a part of her body pressing against him at all times,* MILLA *tears the hem of her nightie. She very capably bandages his arm as she chats.*

[*To* MOSES] Did you see? The figs we picked? You know? [*To* ANNA] Did you show him? [*To* MOSES] Two of them have a little bit of pink on the side…

> *Outside is dawn.*

> *A delivery truck drives by. A song is playing on its radio.*

… this morning. Like a blush it's pretty. Moses.

WHAT THE DEAD SAID TO MILLA: PART 2

MILLA *stumbles a little and* MOSES *catches her.*

MOSES: You right?

MILLA: This is a pigsty that shouldn't be [there]—

> *The song fills the house.*

HENRY: [*to* ANNA] Should we call the police?

> ANNA *watches* MILLA. *She is luminous and dizzy with love.*

ANNA: Not yet… don't call anyone yet

> MILLA *'s stumble turns into a dance.*

And then they said: Dance it Dance it Dance Dance Dance

END OF PART ONE

PART TWO

5.

TILES: THE SHOWER ROUTINE.

ANNA *is showering in the bathroom.* HENRY *is in the kitchen. He is dressed for work.* ANNA *calls out.*

ANNA: Did you shave this morning?

> HENRY *feels his chin.*

HENRY: Uh-huh.

ANNA: What?/ What?

HENRY: / Yes. Yes.

ANNA: Henry?

HENRY: / What?

ANNA: / I don't feel like we ever actively chose these tiles—

HENRY: We did.

ANNA: —this pattern in the tiles? I guess it was just the tiler using his initiative but it's unsettling.

HENRY: Don't let yourself be/ unsettled by the tiles.

ANNA: / There are so many central points he could have chosen for this shaped tile. I don't get why he chose that centre, it's so unset/ tling.

HENRY: / Don't let it be—/ unsettling.

ANNA: / Is there a name for it? This pattern? Henry? [*She waits.*] Are you there?

> HENRY *closes the newspaper he is reading.*

HENRY: I'm seeing Florence today.

> *He drinks a glass of water, standing at the sink. He has a metallic taste in his mouth.*

ANNA: Florence! Ha! What time? What? What time?

HENRY: I'll have to go in a few/ minutes.

ANNA: / Can you just come here and see if we need to call someone in to fix the water pressure?

HENRY: I didn't notice anything—

ANNA: Just tell me if I'm imagining this or if the water pressure's weak.

HENRY: Honestly, I haven't noticed anything. Maybe we need a new showerhead... I'll pay extra attention to it tomorrow. I think it's fine.

ANNA: Just feel/ it now just quickly.

HENRY: / It was fine this morning.

ANNA: Please please just feel it why won't/ you feel it?

HENRY: / Because I did feel it and it was/ fine.

ANNA *charges out, naked and wet, into the kitchen.*

ANNA: [*very casually*]/ Henry, for God's sakes just test the water pressure with my concerns in mind and tell me if it's different. [*She heads back to the bathroom.*] It's such a basic conjugal duty, Jesus.

HENRY *goes into the bathroom. He rolls up his sleeve. He feels the pressure.*

HENRY: Fine. It's fine.

ANNA: Really? Wait—Oh. I thought... [*Genuinely surprised*] Are you going?

HENRY: You cannot lose it yet.

ANNA: [*without much conviction*] I was just concerned about the plumbing and thought: if we have to get men in then better before we start the next round surely? Better we fix this pressure before Wednesday?

HENRY *has a drink of water from the cup full of toothbrushes.*

HENRY: Are you going to get back in or shall I/ t[urn it off?]

ANNA: / No no... I'll...

ANNA *nods looking at the stream of water as if it were a skipping rope—as if with the right timing she could slip in without disturbing the stream of droplets.*

HENRY: It's such a waste of water, Anna.

ANNA: It's too soft, Henry. The water on my back.

HENRY: Are you just going to leave it running?

ANNA: Pass me— [*She points to a cylinder of talcum powder.*] Henry I know. I know I'm starting to smell like an animal. I smell like a pig. Riding a goat or... I don't I honestly don't recognise what animal this is but I can smell her. I haven't gotten past here since Thursday. Y— [*genuinely surprised*] —you're going?!

HENRY: I have to, Anna.

He leaves the bathroom. She follows him.

I'll call this afternoon.

ANNA: I got talc on your lapel.

She tries to get it off.

Sorry. Oh… Sorry. God. Sorry. Sorry. Oh no. Take it off.

She tries to get him out of it. HENRY *catches her wrists.*

HENRY: You know what this is? It's just grief, Anna. This is just grief. And you cannot, cannot, cannot let it—

ANNA: No. [*She closes her eyes.*] You're going—

HENRY: Yes. I have to work.

He leaves. ANNA *is left holding the jacket.*

HENRY LEAVES FOR WORK. TOBY IS LOOKING UP, HER LEFT HAND ON HER BELLY.

TOBY: How did those red sneakers get on the telephone line?

HENRY *squints.* HENRY *and* TOBY *stare up. A bird shadow passes over them.* TOBY *looks at* HENRY *as he looks at the shoes. When he turns to her she looks up again.*

Look at this blue sky blue sky blue sky.

WHEN MOSES SAW ANNA (MEANWHILE IN THE HOUSE).

The door to the bathroom is slightly ajar. MOSES *walks past and* ANNA *washes her face and armpits. She sees him and closes the door.*

HENRY LEAVES FOR WORK. TOBY IS LOOKING UP, HER LEFT HAND ON HER BELLY: PART 2.

TOBY: Does your daughter go to the school on Christy?

HENRY *nods. He stands. He picks up his briefcase.*

I saw you there yesterday.

HENRY: Yesterday? Nnnnnnnn[o]—

TOBY: It was. I'm pretty/ sure.

HENRY: / Oh! That's [right]— I I thought I was meant to pick her up but— We had a little mix-up…

He gets distracted by a possible trajectory for the shoes.

TOBY: I couldn't work out if it was you at first. I know your car but…

They both look at the sneakers.

… you didn't look like/ a a human.

HENRY: / A Henry? Oh. A human.

TOBY: Mmm. Or maybe. It was like you couldn't get the sound out.

Both take a shallow breath.

[*Not looking at him*] You okay?

HENRY *rubs his chest like it hurts.*

HENRY: Just a bit late—

TOBY: / Is that guy your dealer?

HENRY: Guy—

TOBY: That guy at your house.

HENRY: No is he my dealer? No.

TOBY: I know someone who wants to fuck him up pretty bad.

HENRY: I'm sure.

TOBY: If he is your dealer it's cool. Like—

HENRY: He's not my dealer. He's my daughter's… friend. He cut her hair a little while back. And now he—he's staying with us for a while. They're friends and he's— [*His voice hard*] What were you doing up there?

TOBY: What d'you/ mean?

HENRY: / At the school.

TOBY: Looking for—for my dog. I thought I'd just go round the block. But then I just kept going.

HENRY: Toby, that's a very unpleasant walk.

TOBY: I couldn't stop. I can hardly move today. Look.

HENRY: Your—! [*Recoiling at her feet*] You didn't wear shoes?!

TOBY: They don't fit 'cause I'm so—look at my fucking ankles. Look look at me! I'm so fucking pregnant, Henry.

HENRY: You walked all the way up to Christy without shoes?

TOBY: I wanted to find him.

HENRY: You have to use some common sense, Milla.

TOBY: Toby.

HENRY: Y—/ yes.

TOBY: / You called me Milla. I wasn't spying on you. I didn't mean to walk that far.

HENRY: You should've— I could've given you a lift back. I want you to get some antiseptic onto those.

TOBY *shrugs.*

Promise me—
TOBY: Toby.

HENRY *looks at her blankly.*

HENRY: Yes.

He starts leaving.

TOBY: H—Henry... how 'bout that sky? [*Speaking softly so her belly doesn't hear*] Trying to give him something to look forward to. [He's] freaking out a bit.

HENRY *and* TOBY *take each other in.*

[*Unsure*] How 'bout that sky?
HENRY: This? [*Rubbing his chest painfully*] This is a hell of a sky! A hell of a sky.

MILLA AND MOSES EAT FIGS IN THE KITCHEN.

MILLA: Is yours okay?
MOSES: Bit dry. It's sort of T! numbing my/ tongue.
MILLA: / T! Yeah, T! Sappy.
MOSES: How's that?
MILLA: T!

MOSES *takes it from her.*

Thank you.

MOSES *throws both figs out the window.*

Thank you. T!
MOSES: T!

The home phone rings. MILLA *and* MOSES *both jump back.* MOSES *fumbles for a cigarette.* ANNA, *purposefully avoiding looking at* MOSES *walks through to answer it.*

ANNA: We're a non-smoking house. Moses.
MOSES: Yeah right/ sorry.

... MEANWHILE HENRY AT WORK.

HENRY *puts framed photos into his top drawer and locks it with a key in his top left shirt pocket. He takes off his watch. He takes off his shoes and neatly rolls his socks into them. He places them facing forward.*

... GIDON, SHIRTLESS, CALLS ANNA FROM UNIT 48, FIFTH FLOOR, OVERLOOKING THE GARDEN BY THE BINS. HE PLAYS PIANO (INSTRUCTIVELY FOR THUONG) WITH ONE HAND, HOLDING THE RECEIVER IN THE OTHER. ANNA ANSWERS IN HER KITCHEN AND DOES SOMETHING ROMANTIC WITH HER FEET. THUONG PRACTISES VIOLIN IN UNIT 47. MOSES NOTICES THAT MILLA AND ANNA FLUSH IN THE SAME WAY.

ANNA *answers the phone.*

ANNA: / Anna Finlay speaking.
GIDON: Yes.
ANNA: Yes?
GIDON: Anna—my mouth is full. Sorry. I just…
ANNA: Gidon?
GIDON: Mmm!

> ANNA *watches* MOSES *and* MILLA.

Anna—tell me— [*swallowing*] 'scuse me— How is Milla?
ANNA: Well, we're going to do another round of of treatment which the doctors are very positive about so—

> *Pause.*

GIDON: Hello?
ANNA: It's been a strain on her body but we're feeling good about… Sorry. Excuse me a second, Gidon— [*Covering the mouthpiece*] Moses that's blowing inside. Get further outside. [*Returning to the phone*] Sorry.
GIDON: And is Milla playing the violin. At the moment?
ANNA: Not really. It's still very painful with that movement so—

> MILLA *rolls her eyes.*

GIDON: Will you… would *you* please come to my home, Anna?
ANNA: Oh—

GIDON: Will you, Anna,/ please?

ANNA: / Um…

GIDON: I have something I need to ask you.

ANNA: Oh I/ see…

> GIDON *bangs on the adjoining wall with unit 47.*

GIDON: / *Lieliska spelesana!* [Brilliant!]

ANNA: I don't know if I can come any time soon. But—

MILLA: Yes/ you can.

GIDON: / When you have some time. When you have time I will—I will be so happy to seeing you, Milla's mum.

ANNA: I'll I'll call before if I/ find a spare—

GIDON: / Or turn up is easy— Whenever you like! [*Banging on the wall*] Elbow up!

> ANNA *nods and puts down the phone.* MOSES *grins at her.*

ANNA: What?

MOSES: Nothing.

ANNA: No what?

MOSES: Milla does that too.

> *He points out what she has just been doing with her feet.* ANNA *is suddenly aware her manner is a little vivid.*

ANNA: Have you put something in your tummy yet, Mill?

MILLA: Yeah.

> ANNA *gets some medication from the fridge. Notices the box is near empty. She gives* MILLA *her dose.*

ANNA: Moses, I'm going to have to ask you to let me know when you reach the last few of anything Milla's taking.

MOSES: What?

ANNA: [*to* MOSES] I don't know what you'd get out of these but you're obviously getting into them.

MOSES: No.

ANNA: What else?

> MOSES *looks wounded.*

I'm going to have to go out and get more of this before midday so best to let me know now.

MOSES: Maybe bit of—bit of morphine—

ANNA: Okay.

ANNA *picks up the phone and starts dialling.*

MILLA: Who you calling?

ANNA: Just your dad. I'm just going to get him to bring home some Ondansentron—

Through the receiver:

ANSWERING MACHINE AT THE CLINIC: You've called the clinic of Dr Henry Finlay—

ANNA *rolls her eyes and hangs up.*

ANNA: Milla—I'm going to go to Dad's clinic to pick up another script. Would you like to/ come with me?

MILLA: / No.

ANNA: I'll just get Mrs Jenkins to pop in while I'm/ out—

MILLA: / We're fine. Mum. Please don't call Mrs Jenkins. That weepy eye of hers is so gross. Please—

ANNA: Don't overdo it.

MILLA: [*very excited*] Okay.

ANNA: Call me if you need anything. If anything happens—

MILLA: It's cool, Mum. Moses knows CPR. He resuscitated someone/ once.

MOSES: / Ex-girlfriend.

ANNA *looks at him for a moment.*

In a club.

ANNA: [*to* MOSES] Water. Crackers. Peppermint tea.

MOSES: Um, Anna— [*picking up two more packets*] maybe some of this one and this one too?

ANNA *looks at* MILLA.

ANNA: Throw them to me?

She grabs at them but they drop to the ground.

MILLA: Mum can't catch.

ANNA *picks them up.* MOSES *goes to help her.*

MOSES: Sorry.

ANNA *exits.*

[*To* MILLA] What?

MILLA: Do you like me?
MOSES: Sure.
MILLA: Sure.
MOSES: I like you.
MILLA: Like, *like* like? Like I know/ that…
MOSES: / Sure I do.

> *He moves to her. She raises onto tiptoes and leans in to kiss him again as he leans forward. They collide.*

MILLA: / Ah!
MOSES: / Shit—

> *She feels the inside of her mouth with her tongue.*

MILLA: Look.

> *She takes* MOSES *' hand and wobbles her little milk tooth with his finger.*

WHY THE ROOF OF HENRY'S MOUTH TASTED LIKE METAL AND SOMETIMES THERE WAS A SOUND IN HIS HEAD LIKE A CHILD HUMMING.

ANNA *rushes into the clinic. The waiting room is empty. She opens the door to Henry's office. There are no photos on his desk.* HENRY *'s shirt is open, his sleeve rolled up. His teeth champ at a belt constricting the blood flow in his left arm. His neck strains with the effort of pulling it tight. There is a needle in his arm. They see each other.* ANNA *backs out. She closes the door.*

ANNA: [*calling out*] No-one on reception.
HENRY: Denise's kids—her twins are sick.
ANNA: Nothing serious I/ hope—
HENRY: / Some tummy bug…

> HENRY *'s hands are trembling as he takes off the strap. He struggles to do up the buttons of his shirt.* ANNA *comes back in.*

ANNA: I just need to get a script for Milla.

> *He tries to find a prescription pad.* ANNA *helps him.*

HENRY: You—your hair looks nice… with the—the layers—bit different—

ANNA: [*pointing to a button*] That one's still—

>*He pauses with his pen.*

I'll fill it in. Henry—

HENRY: I can't talk about this now.

ANNA: Will you come home?

HENRY: Oh…

>*He looks for his watch.*

GIDON BOILS EGGS ON HIS STOVE.

IN THE NEXT ROOM THUONG TIES HIS SHOE LACES AND PICKS UP HIS VIOLIN TO GO TO GIDON'S HOUSE.

IN HENRY'S CONSULTING ROOM.

ANNA *finds his watch and fastens it on his wrist. He grabs her hand.*

HENRY: We're losing her. Aren't we? We're losing her. Anna, what are we going to do?

ANNA: [*his buttons*] You started with the wrong one.

HENRY: What are we going to do?

ANNA: [*his buttons*] Start with this one.

>*He re-buttons up his shirt, looking to her to see if each button and hole match. She kneels down. Finds his neatly rolled socks and pulls them onto his feet.*

One and good …

>*She puts on his shoes and helps him stand. She smooths his hair.*

Go home.

WHEN ANNA VISITED GIDON IN UNIT 48, FIFTH FLOOR, OVERLOOKING THE GARDEN BY THE BINS. PART 3: ANNA WAS GIVEN AN EGG TO PUT IN HER HANDBAG AND THUONG PLAYED SCALES.

Inside unit 48, Roman plays a very simple tune. GIDON *beats time softly.*

GIDON: *Labi! Labi! Labi!* Now… *esi klusu… and labi!* [Good! Good! Good! Now… be quiet… and good!] Roman, this… not so bad. *Es esmu lepns par tevi.* [I'm proud of you.]

ANNA *knocks on the door.*

[*Tapping* THUONG's elbow] Still the lazy… *Ak Dievs*… [Oh God…] [*To* THUONG] Why you stop? Go! Go! Go! *Labi.* [*Opening the door*] Anna— [*Unconsciously undoing his top button*] Anna. Anna. [*Ushering her inside*] Come.

He takes her head in his hands and kisses her forehead.

Come. [*To* THUONG] Why you stopping?

GIDON *clears the piano stool and places* ANNA *on it. Again she ends up facing the keyboard.* GIDON *goes into the kitchen.*

ANNA: [*quietly*] Are you okay?

THUONG *nods.* GIDON *comes in with a large bowl of eggs.* THUONG *finishes his song.*

Wow—it's amazing. Thuong you're amazing—

GIDON: Is natural for him. Is his nature… He is working hard also. Still with this lazy fucking elbow.

THUONG *goes to get an egg.*

First our guest! Sorry. He is like a savage.

ANNA: Thank you, no.

GIDON: No?! Take it for later. Put in your purse.

ANNA *reticently does this.*

Now, Roman, show Anna how hard you work. Scales, and then you will have an egg. If you play well you will have two eggs. No more with this lazy. G! Take *flight!*

THUONG *commences his scales. He plays as they talk.* GIDON *smiles to* ANNA *at* THUONG's *level of concentration. When* THUONG *makes a small error* GIDON *makes a little choking sound as if his egg had a tiny rib bone in it that caught in his throat.*

GIDON: Tell me how is Milla.

GIDON *takes her hand. He kisses it.*

ANNA: We're trying to stay positive at   the

GIDON: [*to* THUONG] More beautiful for the breaking heart in this woman.

ANNA: [*withdrawing her hand*] No no he's so good.

GIDON: I worry.

ANNA: / Why?

GIDON: / Roman! [*To* ANNA] Excuse me. [*To* THUONG, *clipping his head*] Not from the front of head! [*He adjusts his stance. To* ANNA] Sorry, Milla's mum. I worry—you see… He has no violin of his own. He must borrow with mine but then—how long we can do this? I need my violin—is [*hitting his stomach*] my heart, you understand? Are you comfortable there, Anna?

> ANNA *plays middle C.*

You think, Anna… you think Milla will play again—

> ANNA *presses her whole hand onto the keyboard.*

— soon? I think of her little Gliga, maybe it could… maybe he can look after this for… maybe…?

> THUONG *makes several mistakes. They are unmarked by* GIDON.

Anna. Come…

ANNA: You're asking for my daughter's violin.

GIDON: As the borrow. Only as the borrow.

ANNA: No.

GIDON: What use is it lying at home like a little coffin?

> ANNA *stops playing.*

I mean no harm Anna but you don't know—you don't heard it. There is the little human voice inside this violin wanting to cry out.

ANNA: What do you mean I don't heard it?

GIDON: Milla… play it like a machine. Music is not her nature. [*Gesturing to* THUONG] Milla was never/ this. Or—

> *He gestures towards her.*

ANNA: / Why are you saying this?

GIDON: BECAUSE IT'S A WASTE!

ANNA: YES IT'S A WASTE! YES/ YES

GIDON: / Anna—

ANNA: So we can't give up. We can't./ We can't—

GIDON: / Anna is not about the violin for this Milla. Is not. Is never for her— [*To* THUONG] ELBOW!! Firm finger! [*To* ANNA] I am not asking you to give up— Of course you are her mother you must not—

ANNA: You just asked for/ her violin

GIDON: / Is nothing to do with! The violin is not her heart. It is not how she breathes. Music is is your breath—I see! Your hands always clutching—praying don't let me play! Don t let them see my nature. [*Gesturing as if* MILLA *were in the room*] Is her is her nature

ANNA: What? What are you/ saying?

GIDON: / I trying to show/ you—

ANNA: / You're making no sense—

GIDON: No you you are not making sense Anna [*To* THUONG] *Lieliska spelesana!* [Brilliant!] [*To* ANNA] You are tearing apart. But you are trying controllings it all. Milla dyings—it is making me sad. Is so sad! The world is sad. Not because she is this great violin. Milla is the girl with the slouching and the crazy blushing cheek. This being enough tragedy. The world should being sad. The world should stop for you and for her. But you cannot stop it. This life is playing you when you are breaking. Don't resist it make you crazy. Sing. Play. Feel it Anna feel it. [*Gesturing to the piano*] Fuck fuck you scream… Anna— [*Taking her hands*] FUCK BACK—

He tries to put her hands back on the keyboard. She slams down the lid.

Sudz! [Shit!]

Both snatch their hands away just in time. He opens the lid again and forcibly tries to lay her hands down on the keyboard. They struggle.

Come Anna let it—

She pushes his face violently away.

Anna you go? Go then! Go home! Tear down your house!

ANNA *grabs the bowl of eggs and throws it against the wall.*

ANNA: [*to* THUONG] Shut up.

She leaves, slamming the door. THUONG *lowers his bow.*

GIDON: You keep playing. You are the master! *Es esmu lepns par tevi.* [I'm so proud of you.] Thuong Roman you deserve three egg and two coffee.

They look at the eggs on the ground.

THUONG: Yay!

WHEN ANNA RETURNED HOME AND EVERYTHING SHE CARED ABOUT HAD GONE. AND MOSES HELD HER HANDS BECAUSE THEY WERE SHAKING.

ANNA *carries a savagely uprooted plant with blue flowers.*

ANNA: MILLA!!!! MILL—

> MOSES *steps outside.*

MOSES: She's out.

> ANNA *shakes her head.*

Henry came and got her.
ANNA: Did they say where—?

> *He shakes his head.*

When they'll be—? Oh

> *Shakes his head again.*

Can you just um… hold my wrists. I can't seem to stop

> *She shows him her hands. They are shaking. He puts his cigarette in the side of his teeth and takes her wrists.*

Okay. Thanks

> *She releases one of her hands and folds the hair behind her left ear.*

What?
MOSES: Milla does this.
ANNA: They just won't stop. Were you smoking in there?

> MOSES *takes the plant out of her hands. She continues holding out her wrists. He holds her hands instead.*

ANNA: Do I smell?

> MOSES *nods.*

You do too.
MOSES: 'eah

WHAT THE DEAD SAID TO MILLA: PART 3

Milla. This sunset. Feel its rays on your skin?

WHEN HENRY AND MILLA DROVE TO PALM BEACH FOR
THE DAY AND THE SKY WAS FULL OF PAPPUS. TOBY CAME
TOO. SHE SAT IN THE BACK SEAT ON THE WAY THERE AND
SHOTGUN COMING HOME.

MILLA, *very pale, stands in front of a view with* TOBY. *She wears the red sneakers.*

TOBY: [*quietly to* MILLA] At first I thought it was a joke. Like he's very slow. He's a very slow driver.

HENRY: Okay, I'm taking it now. D'you want to smile? Okay— Oh, the light is gorgeous. Okay…

TOBY: D'you wanna photo just Milla? It's weird I'm here. Is it?

> MILLA *screams and suddenly brushes her chin violently. She rips off her t-shirt.* TOBY *screams and leaps back as well.*

MILLA: Oh my god I thought there was something on my chin. Oh my god was there a spider on my face?

TOBY: Sorry, I really hate them. I really…

> MILLA *shudders. She cautiously shakes out her top.*

HENRY: I think it was just dandelion snow.

> MILLA *shudders again and looks around. The air is full of dandelion parachutes. The light is gold around them.*

Another one with your shirt on?

MILLA: Don't let that end up on the internet.

HENRY: D'you want to smile?

MILLA: Dad.

TOBY: Are you smiling? Let's pout. Shall we pout? Are you pouting? What are/ you doing?

> *The light streams in through the clouds.*

HENRY: / You okay?

MILLA: I think I might need…

HENRY: Is it bad? Is it bad? You want/ water?

MILLA: / Can I have one of the Midazolam, Dad?

HENRY: It's a bit early.

> *He gives her a bottle of water. She retches.*

MILLA: I'm so tired, Henry.

HENRY: How about that cloud over there. Incredible, isn't it? It's so gold. Here.

He gives her a tablet.

You're gonna throw up?

MILLA: Yeah.

HENRY: Wait till that passes. Look at the horizon.

She takes the tablet.

MILLA: [*to* HENRY] I'll take your photo. Toby, stand next to him.

TOBY: You don't need me in your family album. I'm hardly... it's a bit/ weird.

MILLA: / No it's not.

TOBY: Take one of just your dad.

HENRY: That would be a/ waste of film.

MILLA: / Come on. Come on.

HENRY: [*showing* MILLA *the camera*] You focus the depth with that one and that's for the finer focus there... See how the details leap out... See...

MILLA: Mmmm. Okay...

HENRY: And that's where you wind it on.

MILLA: Yeah yeah.

HENRY: And snap just—

MILLA: I know./ I know that.

TOBY: / She knows.

MILLA *throws up.*

MILLA: It's okay. So... give it to me? Stand over there.

HENRY: It's best probably to have the light behind us...

MILLA: No. Go there... with the ledge behind you.

She holds the camera up. TOBY *puts her arm around* HENRY.

TOBY: Get the shoes in. [*Quietly to* HENRY] Can you try to hide my ankles?

MILLA: Dad. I don't think I can do it again.

HENRY: It's the last—

MILLA: I'm tired, Dad— Okay. So you ready?/ Toby?

TOBY: / Yes.

MILLA: You want to smile?

HENRY: Just give me a second.

She turns the camera straight up.

MILLA: It's so gold. Look at it.

HENRY: I think you'd enjoy becoming part of a sky like this, Mill. My girl.

MILLA: I threw up that pill I think. I think I/ need a—

HENRY: / Okay. Okay, Mill. [*He tears off a piece of bread.*] Have a bit of bread with it. It's good bread… nice and fresh. Okay. You okay?

MILLA *tries to swallow.*

I'm giving you two, Mill. If you had four you'd induce a coma. Five… six would probably… you wouldn't wake up probably.

TOBY: That'd kill you for sure.

HENRY: If you took that many, Mill, if I gave you that many I'd lose my licence. You have so many choices, when it gets too much.

MILLA: Mum/ doesn't—

HENRY: / You don't have to— You don t have to do it for us. We'll have each other.

MILLA: Henry, are you ready?

HENRY: Have you wound it on?

MILLA: Point towards that sunset. So we remember what the photo's of. Otherwise it'll just be another photo of a boring/ drive.

HENRY: / Boring?

TOBY: Sorry. I had the stares. I get carsick in the back.

MILLA: You weren't boring, Toby. Point, Henry, point. And look at the sky.

HENRY: / What d'you mean boring?

MILLA: You just drive so slow.

HENRY: Safe.

MILLA: But everyone wants to run you off the road when you're going forty-seven. That's not safe.

HENRY: I don't go forty-seven. I almost always maintain fifty—over fifty. You're only thinking corners.

TOBY: Henry—you go fifteen on corners.

HENRY: I'm/ safe.

TOBY: / But you make everyone around you go loco.

HENRY *laughs.* MILLA *takes the photo.*

MILLA: It's of the sky, remember that one. Not just your finger. [*Winding the camera on*] I'm taking another one. Put your arms around her.
HENRY: Is that okay, Toby?

> TOBY *nods.*

MILLA: Relax, Dad. You look so tense. Look at his/ shoulders.
HENRY: / Well, Toby might not/ like being manhandled.
TOBY: / I like it.
MILLA: Put your hands on her tummy.
TOBY: Go on.

> *He puts his arms around her.*

> [*Very quietly to him*] Can you feel that?

> HENRY *nods.*

I think that's his foot and that's his—look at that—that's his bum—

WHEN THE HOUSE IS EMPTY AND TIME STILL PASSES FOR A MOMENT.

The kitchen is empty. A tap drips.

POST MAGNA.

It is night time. MILLA *sits at the table.* HENRY *stands. He has sweated profusely in the last hour.* ANNA *has wet hair. She is dressed in clothes she hasn't worn for some time. The hanger imprints are on the shoulders and peg creases where they hung on the line.*

HENRY: No-one was/ hurt.
ANNA: What do you mean no-one was/ hurt?
HENRY: / We're all okay. No-one's/ injured.
MILLA: / It was brilliant, Henry. He totally put his foot down Mum. Where's/ Moses?
HENRY: / No-one was injured, Anna.
MILLA: That Magna was/ pretty trashed—
ANNA: / You hit another vehicle!?
MILLA: We just swiped it./ Mum—where's Mo, Mum?
ANNA: [*to* HENRY]/ You shouldn't have been driving at all.
MILLA: God. He's just slow. He's not like/ retarded.
ANNA: [*to* HENRY]/ You know what I mean.

HENRY: They *goad*/ ed me, Anna.

MILLA: / No we/ didn't! We didn't, Mum—

ANNA: / What are you? Fourteen? How fast were you going?

MILLA: He was very much in control until the Magna, Mum.

ANNA: How fast were you going?

HENRY: Forty-eight

ANNA: Forty-eight?

HENRY: Yeah

ANNA: Kilometres?

MILLA: Mum—where's Moses?

ANNA: Um—he just went out for a bit.

MILLA: Did he say when he was gonna/ come back?

HENRY: / It was on a corner

ANNA: It's still not that/ fast.

HENRY: / I wasn't expecting it to be parked/ there—

MILLA: / Mum? Did/ he—?

ANNA: / He won't be long. Did you leave a note?

HENRY: Um—

MILLA: We pulled a hit and run.

ANNA: / Henry!

TOBY: [*offstage*] / Henry!

HENRY: They goaded/ me Anna!

TOBY: [*offstage*] / Henry!/ Henry!

ANNA: How old are you?

> TOBY *stands at the front of the house.*

TOBY: / Henry—

HENRY: / Toby!

> HENRY *goes to the door.*

ANNA: Jesus/ really?

TOBY: Can you take me to the, um, hospital. I'm, um— My waters broke and… It was more than I expected and—

HENRY: Breathing.

TOBY: It's pretty in/ tense.

HENRY: / Breathing. Breathing. Good. D'you know how long/ ago your last—

TOBY: [*breathing intensely*]/ Can you take me now? I know these/ questions are reallllly normal…

HENRY: / You don't want to be waiting around at the hospital if… We'd better/ time the—

    She stops and breathes with huge focus. ANNA *comes to the door.*

ANNA: Oh god don't push are you pushing? Don't let her/ push—

HENRY: / Okay. Let's get you to the/ hospital. [*To* ANNA] You agree? The collision—

ANNA: Go, I think go. Are you okay/ to drive?

HENRY: / I think so.

ANNA: You be careful. Your driving's probably what broke her/ waters in the first place.

TOBY: / PLEASE LET'S GO—

HENRY: Can I take your/ car?

ANNA: / Is yours undrive/ able?

HENRY: / Where are the keys?/ Not at all—

ANNA: / They should be in my bag. [*To* TOBY] You're doing so well.

TOBY: JESUS/ JESUS CHRIST… JESUS CHRIST!

HENRY: / Where's—?

ANNA: / Hanging on the back of the/ door— [*To* TOBY] Shall I call your mum—?

HENRY: / Got it. [*Feeling inside her bag*] Why've you got an egg here?

TOBY: [*to* ANNA] No no, don't! But if Henry… if my dog—

ANNA: We'll take care of/ him

TOBY: / There's/ treats in— [the pantry]

    HENRY *puts the egg on the table.*

HENRY: / Okay Toby. Anna's going to help you/ stand up— You got your overnight—

ANNA: [*swinging the bag over her shoulder*] Yes—/ I'll reverse it out. Throw them—

    He throws the car keys to her. ANNA *doesn't catch them.*

MILLA: [*to* TOBY] / Good luck

HENRY: She won't need luck. She'll be/ fine.

TOBY: / FUCK!… Oh no… that's—

    HENRY *puts his arm around* TOBY *and supports her out.*

—in the pantry—

MILLA: Okay—

HENRY *looks back.* MILLA *is slumped at the table.*

See ya.

HENRY *looks at her.*

TOBY: OH MY GOD!!! Oh my…

MILLA *raises her hand.*

MILLA: 'Bye. You better—

HENRY *pulls towards* MILLA.

ANNA: [*offstage*] Okay—let's go!

ANNA *runs in.*

Car's running…

As she exits:

Now no/ goading d'you hear? You have to be—
[*Offstage, increasingly distant and punctuated by car doors slamming*]
—careful Henry— No giving into… peer group pressure— [*To* TOBY]
Okay… that's good. Great.

MILLA *stands but suddenly grips the back of the chair.*

MILLA: / Whoa… [*Sitting dizzily, she calls out*] You'll be great Toby!

Another distant contraction.

MILLA *rests her head in her hands. She sits in silence for a
moment. Her breathing is laboured. Her hands are shaking. She
looks terrified.* MOSES *appears in the doorway. He stubs out his
cigarette before entering. Sits opposite her.* MILLA *looks up and
smiles.*

Where've you been?

MOSES: Nowhere. I didn't think you'd be gone that long.

They smile at each other.

ANNA: [*coming back into the kitchen*] Your dad's taken off at fift[een]—

She stops when she sees MOSES.

MILLA: I'm gonna lie down, Mum.

ANNA: Yes.

MILLA: [*standing dizzily*] Whoa.

ANNA *stands to support her.*

ANNA: I hope it's not/ concussion.

MILLA: / We hardly even touched the Magna. It was just 'cause, Henry—
[*Suddenly very woozy*]/ Woooo!

ANNA: / Sweetheart./ Come on—

MILLA: / Moses can take me, Mum. You can take me, can't you?

> MOSES *stands. He nods.* ANNA *smiles at* MOSES *as if hiding her teeth.*

ANNA: Milla—

> MILLA *is curled into* MOSES. *He takes her into the bedroom.* ANNA *peels the egg and puts the whole thing in her mouth at once. Then wraps her arms around her body and plays her ribs like ivories.* MOSES *leans out of the room.*

[*Her mouth full*] Does she need/ anything?

> MOSES *looks to* MILLA.

MILLA: [*from inside the room*] It's okay.

> MOSES *closes the adjoining door.*

MILLA AND MOSES GET READY FOR BED.

Stars shimmer at windows, in the doorway. MILLA *and* MOSES *lie in the darkness.* MILLA *lies with her eyes open. A mobile phone beeps.*

MILLA *sits up and pours herself a glass of water. She drinks it.*

MILLA: [*quietly, middle-of-the-night voice*] Mo.

> MOSES *stirs.*

Mo. D'you want to get it on?

> MOSES, *still asleep, laughs.*

Do you? Are you awake?

> *She hits him.*

MO!

MOSES: Wha—? What? You want your dad?

MILLA: No. I want to have sex. D'you want to?

MOSES: Ummm.

MILLA: Did you take some morphine Mo? Did you?

MOSES: Um. Yeah.

MILLA: Oh.

> *He pulls her into him.*

MOSES: But we can do other stuff. D'you want to do other stuff?

MILLA: I don't think I can take another morning. Mo?

MOSES: You want morphine? I can get you a little hit? Yeah?

MILLA: No.

MOSES: Don't think about morning.

MILLA: Mo. Will you do something?

MOSES: You want me to get your dad?

MILLA: No. So don't get weird about this, okay? [*She props herself up on her elbows, idicating a pillow.*] Can you take this and hold it over my face. When my body starts to tense or um when my body starts to kick with something that feels like I've changed my mind, push harder. That's what bodies do apparently they do that. Something fights. But it's not me. Lean in. Don't leave it unfinished. And um wait till my hips drop open. And there's no hold in my spine. Then you can take the pillow away.

> *There is silence.*

Are you pretending to be asleep?

> *A mobile phone beeps with a text message.*

Were you texting?

MOSES: No. Why d'you want to do it like this?

MILLA: It's too much.

MOSES: Get your dad to give you too much morphine.

MILLA: He said this way's better.

> *The phone beeps again.*

MOSES: [*to the phone*] Fuck off.

> *He throws his phone away.*

MILLA: You can call her when it's done.

MOSES: Who?

MILLA: I read your messages Mo. She sure knows a lot of abbreviations.

MOSES: Fuck.

> *Silence.*

Why are you asking me to do this?

MILLA: I can't keep waking up, Mo. I can't. I can't breathe. I know what happens now. From now. My—this body, it's too much. And it just gets more painful. I c— You can leave but p   p   pl   Mo…

MOSES: I won't leave you.

MILLA: Please. I need you to help me. I love you. Don't think. Just help me go.

She takes a pillow from under his head and settles back. She arranges herself painstakingly.

Okay?

She kisses him.

You're doing this because I love you and I want it. Don't stop pushing down. Your body has to bear me down.

MOSES *has a drink of water, places the glass back on the bedside table.*

Can I have a sip?

He hands it to her, watches her drink, replaces it. She places the pillow back over her face. MOSES takes the edge then pushes down for what seems like an unbearably long time. After a while MILLA's body fights. Her arm strikes his back. It hits him and hits him. And then she is screaming. She screams and screams, smothered by the pillow, screaming for her life. He keeps pushing.

MOSES: Milla—shhhh.

Suddenly her body pushes him with a enormous force. She sits, gasping for breath. She fights for more and more air in her lungs. Then grabs him and forces him onto her. She pulls his body onto hers and kisses him hard.

MILLA: Ow.

MOSES: You okay?

MILLA: Yes… my tooth…

She slips something into the glass of water beside the bed that drops like a small pearl to the bottom of the glass.

Sorry.

He pulls her back to him and they make love with great intensity, kissing and breathing and shaking.

Outside a bird calls. It is the first bird before morning. MOSES *climaxes in a shudder.*

MOSES: You o/ kay?

MILLA: / I have to go to the toilet.

MOSES: I'll turn on the light?

MILLA: No.

WHAT THE DEAD SAID TO MILLA: PART 4.

They said: Let go. Let it all go.

6.

WHEN THE HOUSE IS EMPTY AND TIME STILL PASSES.

The kitchen is empty. A tap drips. Murmurs of people talking but the house seems empty. The light in the house is from something un-daylight and un-electric. It's yellow. It's not without intent. And time is passing the way it always does.

HENRY *comes home from the hospital. He is exhausted but radiant. He goes inside. As he enters darkness falls in the house.*

7.

ANNA'S TIME OUTSIDE BEFORE SHE FOUND MILLA (SEEN FROM THE GARDEN).

ANNA: [*offstage*] Onetwothreefour joking Henry. I'm joking.

> *She walks into the back garden with a glass of water and a cracker. The garden is hung with low-lying mist.* ANNA *eats the cracker quickly. She goes back inside.* MOSES *appears at the door, smoking.*
>
> *From outside the dialogue seen in the opening sequence is overheard.*

HENRY: I know how much you mean to her and I'm grateful.

ANNA: [*knocking and opening the door*] Sweetheart. Sweetheart…

HENRY: Please don't hurt her any more than— I know it means nothing from me but, Moses, I'm begging you, I'm—

From offstage, we hear an intaken breath from ANNA. *And then another.* MOSES *takes out another cigarette.* ANNA *enters the room. She stands silently, looking at* MOSES.

ANNA: She's still warm.

    HENRY *leaps up and rushes to the bedroom.*

You left her when/ she was still warm and you.

MOSES: / She was dead already. I woke up and she was already dead. She looked peace/ ful—

ANNA: / NOT NOW SHE DOESN'T! SHE DOESN'T LOOK SO PEACEFUL NOW WITH HER EYES ROLLED BACK LIKE THAT!

MOSES: I closed/ them.

ANNA: / THEY OPENED! WHY DIDN'T YOU CALL ME? WHY DIDN'T YOU TELL ME? WE COULD HAVE RESUSCITATED HER MAYBE SHE'D STILL... MAYBE... maybe— We didn't say goodbye.

MOSES: She was dead, she was already dead.

ANNA: STOP SMOKING IN MY HOUSE, YOU... FUCK!

    She hits his chest.

I DIDN'T SAY GOODBYE! SHE DIDN'T SAY GOODBYE TO ME!

    MOSES *stops protecting himself.* ANNA *beats and beats his chest.*

YOU COME HERE AND YOU SMOKE US OUT AND YOU COME HERE AND YOU USE HER UP, YOU'RE THE ONE WITH THE LAST WORDS WHO GETS TO HOLD HER HAND WHO GETS TO HOLD HER AND YOU USE IT ALL UP

    HENRY *comes in.* ANNA *keeps beating at* MOSES. HENRY *sits.*

HENRY: Anna. He's not responsible. Anna. Anna. Anna/ Anna

    When she has exhausted herself she drops her arms and her knees buckle.

MOSES: Sorry. Sorry. I'm sorry.

    He tries to help her up. ANNA, *without looking at him, fights him off.* HENRY *wearily moves* MOSES *to the side and helps* ANNA *stand.*

HENRY: Come on.

    ANNA *walks slowly outside.*

MOSES: I'm sorry. Anna.

ANNA *is in the garden. She falls to her knees. She looks in the window and sees* HENRY *hugging* MOSES. HENRY'*s shoulders shudder. Her hands are fists on the earth. She pushes them hard into the ground.*

MILLA: **Open your hand, Mum.**

ANNA *sits up. Her fists still tight. Brushes the hair from her forehead, leaving a streak of dirt. Closes her eyes.*

Oh, look!

ANNA *looks up, her eyes still closed.*

A cloud like a ... I don't know. Just a cloud. Isn't it? But very white.

ANNA *opens her eyes.*

I guess it could be a dragon. Or... I keep coming back to the fact it looks like a cloud.

ANNA *is very still.*

8.

THE NEW WORLD.

GIDON *and* THUONG *play a duet.* GIDON *plays the piano badly. The fan is on. There is a roast chicken on the table with half the ribs exposed where the flesh has been torn off.*

ANNA *enters. She carries Milla's violin case. She places the case on the table. Opens it. She pulls a drumstick from the chicken on the table, sits at the piano and eats.*

ANNA, *wipes her hands on her clothes.*

GIDON *takes the little Gliga violin from the case and fits it under* THUONG'*s chin. It is as if this violin had been made for him.*

GIDON *picks up his instrument and plays with him.*

ANNA *places her hands on the piano. She takes a deep breath. They play and play and play.*

THE END

Belvoir presents

BABYTEETH

By **RITA KALNEJAIS**
Director **EAMON FLACK**

Belvoir's production of Babyteeth *opened at Belvoir St Theatre
on Wednesday 15 February 2012.*

Set Designer **ROBERT COUSINS**
Costume Designer **ALICE BABIDGE**
Lighting Designer **NIKLAS PAJANTI**
Composer **ALAN JOHN**
Sound Designer **STEVE FRANCIS**
Assistant Director **KIT BROOKMAN**
Fight Choreographer **SCOTT WITT**
Stage Manager **LUKE McGETTIGAN**
Assistant Stage Manager **LIZ ASTEY**

With
Toby **KATHRYN BECK**
Anna **HELEN BUDAY**
Thuong **DAVID CARREON / SEAN CHU**
Gidon **RUSSELL DYKSTRA**
Moses **EAMON FARREN**
Henry **GREG STONE**
Milla **SARA WEST**

Production Thanks
Monique Irik, violin teacher; Julie O'Connor;
Airena Nakamura; Liz Scott, DET Arts Unit.

Photography Heidrun Löhr
Design Alphabet Studio

Writer's Note

Rita Kalnejais

When you're nineteen and you meet someone you don't stop to think: this person will change my life. You don't think, when you're walking to the shops on the corner, or seeing them dancing through their living-room window to James Brown, or when you wake up riding shotgun on your way back from the coast while they drive your parents' car – you don't think you'll be holding those moments so preciously years and years later. You don't really think of the future at all.

Between the time of my meeting Jemma at nineteen and her death at twenty-two she took lots of photos, we laughed a lot, took long walks, she kissed people in the sea, rode her bike, drank a lot of tea with her mum, skateboarded, and she left a message with my flatmate to pin on my door that read 'the black panther has eaten the baby seal' (code for something seriously still so cool). She broke up with one of the great loves of her life and met another, painted deep-sea creatures, wore a blue bikini around, and a very soft poncho sometimes. You couldn't tell where she was from. She took breaths that were hard to take; said she was scared. Still got the giggles. Wrote long letters. Sat in the sun. She lived as intensely as she could. And at the hospital surrounded by her family – who were such a love song the way they loved Jem – she wrote a note that didn't seem to make sense at the time. But later that night her sister Kate, exhausted from sitting up for days, saw that it read: 'laugh, dance and play the Beatles', which they took as funeral plans. So that's what we did. Our hearts were breaking and we danced to *Good Day Sunshine*. And we felt her sudden distance and wondered how much she'd known and how much she knew now. And looked around at the new world and knew that nothing would be the same again.

Rita Kalnejais

This play isn't about Jemma and her family. It's me trying to understand questions her life asked me. How do you love like you've got nothing to lose? How do you let go? How do you experience the world in all its intensity without being torn apart by its violence and wild, wild, wild kindness? So in week two of rehearsals, having started writing this play a year ago this is how I'm asking this question.

I have a lot of people I want to thank for helping me write this play…

Enormous gratitude to Shyla Mills and Lisa Johnson for your incredible insights and practical medical information.

To Ojars Greste and Aldis Birzulis and Rovena Andruskecica. Also to Erkki Veltheim who talked with me about violins.

Everyone on reception at various clinics I suddenly called for medical details.

Enormous thanks to my parents for their unwavering support, even when I would ring in the middle of the night and ask my dad how to say 'fuck you' in Latvian. Thank you to my mum for being so brave and such a dear friend and putting the lambskin in my bed. And to my sisters Linda and Margaret, and my precious, precious nephew Jason.

Helen Buday for saying: 'Love is more precious than air, more often than not,' and for so many things.

Amelia Best for relentless support and beauty. Alice McConnell. Shon. Lally Katz. Skip.

My literary agents Nellie Flannery and Sally McLennan. And thank you, thank you, thank you to Julie Curran who has been such an incredible hand on my back throughout this process and is dear to my heart.

The actors and creatives in this current production. I'm stunned by you all. Luke McGettigan and Liz Astey. Beautiful Kit Brookman.

Thank you to everyone who has read this script along the way for what you have brought to the play: Alison Bell, Brigid Gallagher,

Jacek Koman, Jackie McKenzie, Kieran Darcy-Smith, Adam Hatzimanolis, Benedict Samuels, Eloise Mignon.

Huge thanks to Eamon Flack who has supported this script ever since I told him my inciting idea, and for whom I have enormous respect, trust and love. To Anthea Williams for her insights and generosity, Cathy Hunt (always divine), Ralph Myers, Tahni Froudist, Brenna Hobson and everyone at Belvoir who has been so supportive and excellent and entrusting me to write a romantic comedy even when I kept pitching ideas of dogs and death at them. To Bobby Cousins who is always very quietly influential and smart with his instincts.

To Chris Mead, for talking things through with me and always asking the right questions. To Doulla Manolli, a truly brilliant script adviser and friend. And Matthew Whittett, an excellent mind and heart (also Nat and Jasper for fish pie and ninjago insights when I needed them).

Thank you to everyone who has loved me while I've been writing this, especially when I've been so antisocial and hard to be around. To people who I met on the streets and were very wise with me, and honest and generous when I grabbed them to ask about their violin cases or what they'd taken to get so high.

To the man who came to check I was ok when I was lying on the grass who gave me a shock – I didn't mean to scream like that. I know it shook you up. Thank you for checking on me.

To Jemma and her family. To Annabel and Toby.

And also an especial thanks to the boy who, fifteen years ago, sat next to me on the train from Strathfield in the grey hoodie, with the train track of scars up and down his arm. You gave me a little paper crane you made from a torn up catalogue. I was sad that day. Thank you for showing me how to move its wings by pulling its beak and tail.

Director's Note

Eamon Flack

To begin with: Rita Kalnejais. A few years ago she wrote a play, her first, called *B.C.*. It was set in Australia now, and it was a comedy about the immaculate conception, and also a drama about incest and an extended essay on grace. From the first, then, there was no denying it: Rita is a true original. Ralph Myers and I saw Simon Stone's production of *B.C.* in Melbourne (it contained one of the most breathtaking scenes I've ever seen on stage) and began a conversation with Rita about writing a play for Belvoir. She told us she'd like to write a romantic comedy about death, but she was also working on some ideas for a play about dogs. We suggested she take her pick and gave her a contract on spec. A few months later she rang and asked me if I'd like to know what she was writing for us. I was out getting lunch. I said yes and in a long, single breath she described the outline of *Babyteeth* – a girl dying of cancer, a junkie, a mother, a violin teacher… I remember that I stopped in the street by one of those grey electrical boxes and decided it was either brilliant or unlikely, or perhaps both. I also remember that I had never heard anything like it and that I was excited. A few months after that, in February 2011, Rita sent through a first draft. She won't mind me saying that this first draft was a gloriously alive but misshapen thing, glimmering with more human insight than you get in whole novels and throbbing with a sort of naked, newborn determination to grow up and be marvellous. Which, in the remarkably short space of 10 months, thanks to Rita's relentless inquisitiveness, it has done.

Over the last month or so, sometimes from behind our eyelashes and sometimes with bared teeth, Rita and I have had a series of conversations about her play. They have happened where an affair might: over breakfast in Darlinghurst, in the early hours of the new year in Killcare, at dusk in the sand at Shark Bay, late evenings in the office. There has been a lot of tea and chocolate and talk about our various foiled love affairs. I mention this seemingly unnecessary context because the play has always had a two-way infectiousness about it – a resonating way of negating the usual gap between art and living. Now we are in the second week of rehearsals and the whole experience continues to be, like the play itself, and like Rita, its own stream of life – a blinking-in-the-morning-light sort of encounter with the gamut of the world. As we work away it keeps demanding of us that we listen carefully, take care of each other and stand in the face of our fears. It doesn't tolerate slack thinking or shortcuts, and it refuses to accept an estimation, an assumption or a sentimental recourse to obvious beauty. And yet it unashamedly insists on the usefulness of beauty. It never avoids the hard edges and sharp realities of life. It knows that death *shall* have its dominion – that we *live* in death's dominion. But merely taking life seriously is not good enough

Eamon Flack

either: it makes earnestness blush and sometimes even finds the precipice funny. It certainly has time for ridiculousness, and it is fascinated by pettiness and rudeness and manipulation. It is unembarrassed about embarrassment and humiliation and the very earthbound, very flawed nature of the species. It constantly points out, sometimes rudely and sometimes charmingly, that the beauties and consolations and pleasures of life are more widespread than we tend to think they are. It demands that we look at the obvious, the common and the familiar again and again until we see what's really there and what's really going on. But it refuses to spare us the fact that it all ends in pain, fear and dissolution. It's a sort of post-religious boot camp for our spiritual instinct… with a screwball edge.

Which begs the question: is *Babyteeth* a comedy or a tragedy? Or, more importantly, is *life*, ending as it invariably does in *death*, a comedy or a tragedy?

There is a lot of pain in this play. It is interested in what it is like to face oblivion. How does a person leave the world? What does it take to die? When what you've lived by is disintegrating, what do you draw on to continue living? What is living anyway? What is your nature? These are good questions. I like these questions. They cross civilizations. They defy religions and political systems. They're BIG questions – about destiny and one's nature, about grief and loss, about being and sensation, about thought and consciousness. Great and difficult stuff. But what I like most about this play is that its profound and headlong consideration of these questions is built entirely from the familiar matter of daily life. There is almost nothing in the play that doesn't pass us by every day – on the bus, in the living room, at work, in the park. As Milla's life fines down by a process of elimination and obliteration to its essence, and it seems that the fact of death is too much to bear, these characters find themselves drawing deeply on an extraordinary and obvious resource – a kind of catalogue, with infinite entries and infinite details, of reasons and means to remain in the midst of *living*, called the *world*. At the heart of *Babyteeth* is an extraordinarily curious, open and generous way of seeing. It is a reminder that, even in the crammed rooms of the everyday – with all its requirements to drink water, take care of your knees, open and close doors, keep your marriage, sometimes lose a loved one – there are still other dimensions for further living.

But look, if this all sounds a bit too grand – I'm not without that foible – then please ignore it and take away a more succinct thought: *Babyteeth*, like life, and in spite of death, is (probably) a comedy.

Eamon Farren & Sara West

Helen Buday

Greg Stone

Biographies

RITA KALNEJAIS Writer
Rita trained as an actor at the Victorian College of the Arts. As a playwright, her first play, *B.C.*, was produced by The Hayloft Project/Full Tilt at the Melbourne Arts Centre. Her short plays *Whistling in Bed* and *How to Get Very Clean* have been staged as part of Sydney Theatre Company's Rough Draft and Next Stage *Money Shots* respectively. Her acting credits with Belvoir include *The Kiss*, *The Lieutenant of Inishmore*, *A Midsummer Night's Dream*, and for B Sharp *Disco Pigs* (Fresh Track Productions/B Sharp). Other stage credits as an actor include *The Trial*, *Furious Mattress*, *Moving Target* and *Odyssey* (Malthouse Theatre); *Morph, Life Is a Dream* and *Mr Kolpert* (Sydney Theatre Company). Rita was nominated for a 2009 Green Room Award for Best New Writing for the Australian Stage for *B.C.* She is currently a resident playwright at Sydney Theatre Company.

EAMON FLACK Director
Eamon is Associate Director – New Projects at Belvoir. He graduated from the acting course at WAAPA in 2003 and has since worked as a director, actor, writer and dramaturg for Belvoir, Malthouse Theatre, Sydney Theatre Company, Bell Shakespeare's Mind's Eye, ThinIce, Perth International Arts Festival, Darwin Festival, Griffin Stablemates, PlayWriting Australia, ArtRage, Deckchair and various other companies. For Belvoir he directed the final 2011 Season production, *As You Like* It. Also in 2011 he directed *Wulamanayuwi and the Seven Pamanui* for Darwin Festival and his production of *A Midsummer Night's Dream* toured nationally. In 2010 Eamon directed *The End* for Belvoir, which toured to the Malthouse in Melbourne, and he was a special guest at the Alberta Theatre Projects' Enbridge PlayRites Festival in Calgary, Canada. In 2009, Eamon adapted and directed Gorky's *Summerfolk* for Bob Presents and *A Midsummer Night's Dream* for Bob Presents, Arts Radar and B Sharp; his adaptation of Sophocles' *Antigone* was directed by Matthew Lutton for ThinIce and the Perth International Arts Festival; and he was assistant director to Neil Armfield on *The Book of Everything* for Belvoir and Kim Carpenter's Theatre of Image. As dramaturg, Eamon has worked on Belvoir's *Neighbourhood Watch*, *The Wild Duck*, *Gwen in Purgatory* and *The Book of Everything*. He is series editor of Currency Press' Currency Classics, and his adaptation of *Antigone* has been published.

LIZ ASTEY Assistant Stage Manager
Babyteeth is **Liz**'s first production with Belvoir. Her other stage and production management credits include *Wulamanayuwi and the Seven Pamanui* (Darwin Festival); *Goodbye Vaudeville Charlie Mudd* (Malthouse Theatre); *My Girragundji, Soldier Boy* (Canute Productions); *Something Blew* (2nd Toe Dance Collective), *Kassandra, A Doll's House, The Perjured City* and *The Room* (Victorian College of the Arts). Liz's event credits include Sydney Festival and Sydney Festival First Night, Darwin Festival and Sydney New Year's Eve.

ALICE BABIDGE Costume Designer
Since graduating from NIDA's design course in 2004, **Alice** has designed costumes and sets for theatre, opera, film and TV. She has been the resident designer at Sydney Theatre Company for the last two years. For Belvoir Alice created the costumes for *That Face*, *Who's Afraid of Virginia Woolf?*, *Parramatta Girls* and *Capricornia*. Her other costume credits include *Gross und Klein*, *True West*, *The Trial*, *Honour*, *The War of the Roses*, *The Season at Sarsaparilla*, *The Lost Echo*, *Boy Gets Girl*, *Julius Caesar* (Sydney Theatre Company). Alice designed both sets and costumes for *The White Guard, Next Stage Shorts, The Oresteia, The Women of Troy* (Sydney Theatre Company); *Self Esteem* (Wharf 2LOUD);

King Tide, The Nightwatchman, The Peach Season, Strangers in Between (Griffin Theatre Company); *Weather* (Railway Street Theatre Company); *The Drowned World* (Darlinghurst Theatre); *Jumping and All That* (Big Shoes Theatre Company); *The Share, The Hour Before My Brother Died* (Old Fitzroy Theatre) and the opera *The Navigator* (2008 Brisbane Festival). She created the sets for *The Mysteries, The Year of Magical Thinking* and *The Wonderful World of Dissocia* (Sydney Theatre Company). Alice has designed music video clips for artists such as The Mess Hall, End of Fashion and You Am I, and works on film projects and TV commercials with Cherub Pictures. She most recently co-designed the costumes for the feature film *Snowtown*. Alice's work also includes costumes for the operas *Caligula, The Return of Ulysses* (English National Opera); *Rigoletto* (Komische Oper, Berlin); *The Marriage of Figaro* and *Bliss* (Opera Australia). Alice won the 2011 Sydney Theatre Award for Best Costume Design for *Gross und Klein*.

KATHRYN BECK Toby

Kathryn graduated from the Queensland University of Technology in 2006. Her theatre credits include *King Tide* (Griffin Theatre Company); *Lion on the Streets, Once in a Lifetime, Our Country's Good, Twelfth Night* and *Terrain, Terrain, Terrain* (Queensland University of Technology). For film, Kathryn's credits include *Not Suitable for Children, Burning Man, The Little Things, Subdivision* and *Mosaic*. Her television credits include *All Saints, East of Everything, Scorched, Chandon Pictures* and *Home and Away*. Kathryn received an AFI Award nomination in 2009 for Best Supporting Actress in a Television Drama for *Scorched*, and in 2007 a Sydney Theatre Award nomination for Best Newcomer for *King Tide*.

KIT BROOKMAN Assistant Director

Kit trained as an actor at NIDA, graduating in 2008. He wrote and directed *Heaven* (NovemberISM at the Old 505 Theatre). As an actor his stage credits include *Twelfth Night* (Bell Shakespeare Company); *A Midsummer Night's Dream* (Bob Presents/Arts Radar/B Sharp); *The Royal Seed* (Sydney Opera House); *DNA* (Spiky Red Things/Old Fitzroy). For radio he has performed in *Hamlet* (ABC Radio National), and for television in *Micronation*. Kit's play *Close* was shortlisted for the 2010 Griffin Award and the 2011 Patrick White Young Playwright's Award. *Heaven* was presented at the 2011 National Play Festival. Kit was shortlisted for the 2011 Inscription/Albee Foundation Award. He is currently a PlayWriting Australia associate playwright at Belvoir.

HELEN BUDAY Anna

Helen graduated from NIDA in 1983. For Belvoir her credits include *A Midsummer Night's Dream, The Threepenny Opera, The Marriage of Figaro*, and *A Doll's House* for which she won the Sydney Critics' Circle Best Actress Award. Other theatre credits include *Dirty Dancing* (Jacobsen Entertainment); *Company, Skylight, High Society, The Importance of Being Earnest* (Melbourne Theatre Company); *Macbeth, The Threepenny Opera, Uncle Vanya, Racing Demon, The Revengers Tragedy, Once in a Lifetime, A Midsummer Night's Dream, The Marriage of Figaro, The Country Wife, Pericles, The Seagull, Pillars of Society* (Sydney Theatre Company); *Kate'N'Shiner* (Deckchair Theatre Company); *After Dinner* (Black Swan State Theatre Company); *Crazy for You* (Gordon Frost); *Head of Mary, The Incorruptible* (Playbox Theatre); *The Emerald Room, Cosi, School for Scandal, High Society, Cabaret* (State Theatre Company of South Australia); *Crimson Island, The Three Sisters, Macbeth, The Wolf's Banquet* (Anthill Theatre Company); and *My Fair Lady* (Victorian State Opera). Her TV credits include *All Saints, Stingers, Secrets, Land of Hope, Five Mile Creek* and *Shadow of the Cobra*. Helen's film credits include Alexandra's *Project, Dingo, For Love Alone* and *Mad Max: Beyond Thunderdome*. Her role in *Alexandra's Project* earned her the Best Actress Award at the Valladolid International Film Festival in Spain. Helen is director of Le Bout du Monde, an annual Australian film festival, held in the south of France in May. She has performed in *Le Dindon* and *Georges Dandin*, and choreographed *Cendrillon* for Illustre Théâtre in Pézenas, France.

DAVID CARREON Thuong
David is 11 and started playing violin at the age of four. He currently plays with the Symphony Orchestra in the NSW Public Schools Arts Unit, as well as with the Peter Seymour Orchestra and TangoOz ensemble in the Sydney Youth Orchestras. He has completed his AMEB Grade 8 practical exam (for piano and violin) and is preparing for the Associate Diploma (AMusA) for both. David has won prizes in eisteddfods throughout Sydney.

SEAN CHU Thuong
Sean makes his Belvoir debut with *Babyteeth*. He is Japanese-Malaysian and was born in Hong Kong in 2001. Sean moved to Sydney with his family in 2007 and started playing the violin in 2008, under the Suzuki violin program, which fostered his love for music. He is currently a Year 6 student and is involved in numerous musical groups. Sean has performed in various school and Suzuki concerts.

ROBERT COUSINS Set Designer
For Belvoir, **Robert** has designed sets for *Cloudstreet, Page 8, As You Like It, Twelfth Night, Aliwa, Waiting for Godot, The Threepenny Opera, Gulpilil, A Midsummer Night's Dream* and *Who's Afraid of Virginia Woolf?*. His other design credits include *Julius Caesar, The Season at Sarsaparilla, Art of War, The Serpent's Teeth, The War of the Roses* (Sydney Theatre Company); *The Eternity Man* (Almeida Theatre, London); *Shades of Gray* (Sydney Dance Company); and *Night Letters* (State Theatre Company of South Australia). His set and costumes credits include *Kafka's Metamorphosis, Fat Pig* (Sydney Theatre Company); *House Among the Stars, The Merchant of Venice, Drowning in My Ocean of You* (State Theatre Company of South Australia); *The Dreamed Life* (Comeout01); and *The Duckshooter* (Brink Productions). For film, Robert was production designer on *Candy*, directed by Neil Armfield, *Romulus, My Father*, directed by Richard Roxburgh, and *Balibo*, directed by Robert Connolly. Most recently, Robert wrote and edited *25 Belvoir Street*, a history of the first 25 years of theatre at Belvoir. He is currently designing a production of Wagner's *Ring Cycle* to be presented by Opera Australia in 2013.

RUSSELL DYKSTRA Gidon
For Belvoir, **Russell** has appeared in *Yibiyung, Toy Symphony, Stuff Happens, Ray's Tempest, The Underpants, The Laramie Project* and *The Ham Funeral*. Other credits include *God of Carnage, The Wonderful World of Dissocia; The Unlikely Prospect of Happiness* (Sydney Theatre Company); *Not Like Beckett* (Malthouse Theatre); *The Gypsy Boy* (Theatre of Image); *Below* (Griffin Theatre Company); and *The Imaginary Invalid* (Ensemble Theatre). His television credits include *Wild Boys, Rake, Spirited, My Place, Strike Team, The Adventures of Charlotte & Henry, Blackjack, Loot, All Saints, White Collar Blue, Backberner, Grass Roots, Water Rats* and *Medivac*. For film, Russell has appeared in *Oranges and Sunshine, The View from Greenhaven, Hey Hey It's Esther Blueburger, Romulus, My Father, Clubland, The Wannabes, Ned Kelly, Garage Days, Lantana* and *Soft Fruit*. Russell has received the Helpmann Award for Best Male in a Supporting Role for both *Toy Symphony* and *Stuff Happens*. He also received a Sydney Theatre Award for Best Male in a Supporting Role for *Toy Symphony*. He received an AFI nomination for Best Supporting Actor for *Romulus, My Father*, and received an AFI Award for Best Actor in a Leading Role for *Soft Fruit*.

EAMON FARREN Moses
Eamon graduated from NIDA in 2007. His theatre credits include *Ladybird* (B Sharp/Small Things Productions); *The Beauty Queen of Leenane* (Sydney Theatre Company); *Fugitive* (Windmill Theatre); *The Kid* (Griffin Theatre Company) and various readings and workshops for Belvoir, Sydney Theatre Company and Griffin Theatre Company. Eamon's film work includes *Lucky Country, Red Dog, Blessed* and *X*. He has recently shot John Duigan's upcoming film *Careless Love*, and has a lead role in the upcoming US feature film *Chained*, directed by Jennifer Lynch. Eamon was awarded runner-up in the 2010 Heath Ledger Scholarship.

Eamon Farren

Russell Dykstra

STEVE FRANCIS Sound Designer

Steve is a composer and sound designer who has worked extensively in theatre, dance and screen. As a composer or sound designer for Belvoir he has worked on *The Book of Everything, Gethsemane, The Power of Yes, Ruben Guthrie, Baghdad Wedding, Keating!, Paul, Parramatta Girls, Capricornia, The Spook, Box the Pony, Gulpilil and Page 8*. Other theatre credits include *Bang* (B Sharp/Whitebox Theatre), *Jesus Hopped the A Train* (B Sharp/murri fulla films), *Vital Organs* (B Sharp/Easily Distracted); *Pygmalion, Bloodland, Blood Wedding, The White Guard, The Removalists, Tusk Tusk, Gallipoli, The Great, Rabbit, Pig Iron People, Romeo and Juliet, The Taming of the Shrew, Embers, The 7 Stages of Grieving, Stolen* (Sydney Theatre Company); *This Year's Ashes, Speaking in Tongues, Strange Attractor* (Griffin Theatre Company); *The Suitors, Love and Money* (Old Fitzroy); and *Disarming Rosetta* (Hothouse Theatre). For dance, Steve has composed music for *Belong, True Stories, Skin, Corroboree, Walkabout, Bush* and *Boomerang* (Bangarra Dance Theatre); and *Totem* (Australian Ballet). His recent compositions for the screen include music for *Cops LAC* for Channel 9, the Fox mini-series *Dangerous* and the short films *Dik* and *The Burnt Cork*. His awards include 2003 Helpmann Awards for Best Original Score and Best New Australian Work for *Walkabout*, and a 2011 Sydney Theatre Award for *The White Guard*, with Alan John.

ALAN JOHN Composer

Alan has a long association with Belvoir, composing music for *Summer of the Seventeenth Doll, The Diary of a Madman, The Adventures of Snugglepot & Cuddlepie and Little Ragged Blossom* (with John Clarke and Doug MacLeod), *Peribanez, Stuff Happens, The Chairs, The Spook, Our Lady of Sligo, The Underpants, Waiting for Godot, My Zinc Bed, Emma's Nose, Twelfth Night, The Small Poppies, As You Like It, The Governor's Family, Diving for Pearls, Hate, The Tempest,* and he was musical director for *The Man from Mukinupin*. Other theatre credits include *The White Guard, A Street Car Named Desire, Gallipoli, The Great, Mother Courage, The Season at Sarsaparilla, Hedda Gabler, The Give and Take* (Sydney Theatre Company); *Much Ado About Nothing, The Government Inspector, Romeo and Juliet, Henry V* and *Henry IV* (Bell Shakespeare Company). Major musical works include *The Eighth Wonder* (Opera Australia); *Through the Looking Glass* and *Optimism* for Victorian Opera and Malthouse Theatre. Alan is a sought after composer for the screen, with credits including *Looking for Alibrandi, The Bank, The Shark Net, Three Dollars, Love My Way* and *COPS LAC*. Alan's awards include Helpmann Awards for Best Opera for *The Eighth Wonder* and Best Original Music for *The Diary of a Madman*, APRA Screen Music Awards for *The Shark Net, The Bank, Human Contraptions,* and an AFI Best Music nomination for *Three Dollars*. Alan received a 2011 Sydney Theatre Award for *The White Guard*, with Steve Francis.

LUKE McGETTIGAN Stage Manager

Luke is Belvoir's Resident Stage Manager. For Belvoir he has stage managed *Summer of the Seventeenth Doll, Neighbourhood Watch, The Wild Duck, Namatjira* (Belvoir/Big hART), *Page 8, The End, That Face, The Promise, Scorched, Antigone, Keating!, The Caucasian Chalk Circle* and *The Little Cherry Orchard*. His other credits include *The Pig Iron People, The Give and Take, Bed, La Dispute* (Sydney Theatre Company); *Like a Fishbone* (Sydney Theatre Company/Griffin Theatre Company); *The Government Inspector, The Tempest, The Servant of Two Masters, The Comedy of Errors, The Taming of the Shrew* (Bell Shakespeare Company); *Paradise City, Through the Wire* (Performing Lines); *Alive at Williamstown Pier* (Griffin Theatre Company); *Scam, Abroad With Two Men* (Christine Dunstan Productions); *Flexitime, Market Forces, Shoe Horn Sonata, Blinded by the Sun* (Ensemble Theatre); *The Complete Works of William Shakespeare* (Spirit Productions); *Twelfth Night, Arms and the Man, Much Ado About Nothing, Spring Awakening* (Railway Street Theatre Company); *Barmaids, Radiance* (New England Theatre Company); *My Girragundji* (Canute Productions); and *Dog Logs* (Marguerite Pepper Productions).

NIKLAS PAJANTI Lighting Designer

For Belvoir, **Nik**'s lighting designs include *The Wild Duck, The Promise, Baghdad Wedding, Yibiyung, The Pillowman* and *Who's Afraid of Virginia Woolf?* Other credits include *Spring Awakening* (Sydney Theatre Company); *When the Rain Stops Falling* (Brink Productions/ Sydney Theatre Company); *Kitten* (Jenny Kemp/Malthouse Theatre), *Not Like Beckett* (Malthouse Theatre); *Holiday, Affection* (Ranters Theatre); *Endgame, Othello, The Winter's Tale, King John, The Crucible* (The Eleventh Hour); *Axeman Lullaby* (BalletLab); *Black Marrow, I Want to Dance Better at Parties, Singularity, Tense Dave, Three's a Crowd* (Chunky Move); *Spicks and Specktacular-The Finale, Good Evening, Frank Woodley-Possessed, Lano and Woodley-Goodbye* (Token Events); *Star Voyager-Exploring Space On Screen, Dreams Come True-The Art Of Disney's Classic Fairy Tales, Tim Burton The Exhibition-Melbourne Winter Masterpieces* (Australian Centre for the Moving Image); *The Eye of the Storm* (Fred Schepisi feature film). Nik is principal lighting designer for trafficlight, an independent specialist design and management studio based in Melbourne.

GREG STONE Henry

Greg is a graduate of NIDA. Previously for Belvoir he has appeared in *Stuff Happens*. His other theatre credits include *Clybourne Park, Life Without Me, Poor Boy, Blackbird, Love Song, Assassins, The Pillowman, Cloud Nine, The Seagull, A Little Night Music, Angels in America* (Melbourne Theatre Company); *The Beauty Queen of Leenane, Stones in His Pockets, Merrily We Roll Along* (Sydney Theatre Company); *Don's Party* (State Theatre Company of South Australia); *A Golem Story, Eldorado* (Malthouse); *Wars of the Roses* (Bell Shakespeare); *Julia 3, Myth Propaganda and Disaster in Nazi Germany and Contemporary America, Rapture, A Return to the Brink, Miracles, Good Works* (Playbox Theatre Company); *Who's Afraid of Virginia Woolf?, Life x 3* (Black Swan State Theatre Company); *All the Black Dogs, McNeil* (Griffin Theatre Company); and *The Berry Man* (Hothouse Theatre). Greg's film credits include *Sunset Six, Swerve, Oranges and Sunshine, Van Diemen's Land, Boytown* and *The Bank;* and for TV *Winners & Losers, Lowdown, Underbelly, City Homicide, The Librarians, Blue Heelers, MDA, Stingers, Marshall Law, Halifax f.p., Seachange, Janus, Neighbours, The Man from Snowy River, Phoenix* and *Boys from the Bush*. Greg received a Helpmann award and a Green Room award for *Stuff Happens*.

SARA WEST Milla

Sara graduated with Honours from the Flinders Drama Centre in 2010. Her theatre credits include *Don's Party, Love, Some Girls* (Flinders Drama Centre); *God is Dead* (Stone/Castro) and *Don't Look Back* (Adelaide Bank Festival of the Arts). For film, Sara's credits include *The Turned* and the short films *Collision* and *Spine*.

SCOTT WITT Fight Choreographer

Scott has worked for over 25 years as a fight director, movement consultant, actor, director and clown. As a fight director and movement consultant his theatre credits include *The Dark Room, Summer of the Seventeenth Doll, Gwen in Purgatory, That Face* (Belvoir); *Fool for Love* (B Sharp/Savage Productions); *Spring Awakening, God of Carnage, A Streetcar Named Desire, The Duel, Elling, The Wonderful World of Dissocia* (Sydney Theatre Company); *Taming of the Shrew* (Bell Shakespeare); *Anatomy Titus: Fall of Rome, The Alchemist, Richard III* (Bell Shakespeare/ Queensland Theatre Company); *Toy Symphony, The Crucible, School of Arts, Stones in His Pockets, Who's Afraid of Virginia Woolf?, The Glass Menagerie, The Estimator, Private Lives* (Queensland Theatre Company); *Summer of the Seventeenth Doll, The 48 Shades of Brown, Way Out West, The John Wayne Principle* and *As You Like It* (La Boite).

belvoir 2012

BURIED CITY
6 JANUARY – 5 FEBRUARY BY RAIMONDO CORTESE

I'M YOUR MAN
12 JANUARY – 5 FEBRUARY BY ROSLYN OADES

THYESTES
15 JANUARY – 19 FEBRUARY BY THOMAS HENNING,
CHRIS RYAN, SIMON STONE, MARK WINTER

BABYTEETH
11 FEBRUARY – 18 MARCH BY RITA KALNEJAIS

EVERY BREATH
24 MARCH – 29 APRIL BY BENEDICT ANDREWS

FOOD
26 APRIL – 20 MAY BY STEVE RODGERS

STRANGE INTERLUDE
5 MAY – 17 JUNE BY SIMON STONE AFTER EUGENE O'NEILL

OLD MAN
7 JUNE – 1 JULY BY MATTHEW WHITTET

DEATH OF A SALESMAN
23 JUNE – 12 AUGUST BY ARTHUR MILLER

CONVERSATION PIECE
25 AUGUST – 23 SEPTEMBER BY LUCY GUERIN

PRIVATE LIVES
29 SEPTEMBER – 11 NOVEMBER BY NOËL COWARD

MEDEA
11 OCTOBER – 25 NOVEMBER BY KATE MULVANY &
ANNE-LOUISE SARKS AFTER EURIPIDES

BEAUTIFUL ONE DAY
17 NOVEMBER – 23 DECEMBER BY PAUL DWYER,
EAMON FLACK, RACHAEL MAZA LONG, DAVID WILLIAMS

DON'T TAKE YOUR
LOVE TO TOWN
29 NOVEMBER – 23 DECEMBER BY EAMON FLACK & LEAH PURCELL

Sunday Forum

The bigger picture, the story behind the show, the who's who and the what's what – Sunday Forum is the new window into our work. There'll be a Sunday Forum for every Upstairs show in 2012, at 3pm on the second to last Sunday of the season. Join us in the theatre and we'll have a panel of special guests – performers, creatives, commentators, reviewers, pundits – for a discussion on the show and how it fits into the world at large.

You'll have a chance to ask your burning questions during the forum, and continue the discussion informally with us in the foyer afterwards.

Sunday Forums are free, and you don't need to have seen the show yet to be involved. Each topic will be firmed up once the show opens; check our website or call Box Office for updated information.

See you there!

Bookings are essential and are available four weeks before each forum.
Book: www.belvoir.com.au/sundayforum
or call Box Office on 02 9699 3444.

Babyteeth
Sunday 11 March

Every Breath
Sunday 22 April

Strange Interlude
Sunday 10 June

Death of a Salesman
Sunday 5 August

Conversation Piece
Sunday 16 September

Private Lives
Sunday 4 November

Beautiful One Day
Sunday 16 December

The Belvoir Story

One building.
Six hundred people.
Thousands of stories.

When the Nimrod Theatre building in Belvoir Street, Surry Hills, was threatened with demolition in 1984, more than 600 people – ardent theatre lovers together with arts, entertainment and media professionals – formed a syndicate to buy the building and save this unique performance space in inner-city Sydney.

Over 25 years later, this space, known as Belvoir St Theatre, continues to be the home of one of Australia's most celebrated theatre companies – Belvoir. Under the artistic leadership of Ralph Myers and General Manager Brenna Hobson, Belvoir engages Australia's most prominent and promising playwrights, directors, actors and designers to realise an annual season of work that is dynamic, challenging and visionary. As well as performing at home, Belvoir regularly takes to the road, touring to major arts centres and festivals both nationally and internationally.

Both the Upstairs and Downstairs stages at Belvoir St Theatre have nurtured the talents of many renowned Australian artists: actors including Geoffrey Rush, Cate Blanchett, Toby Schmitz, Robyn Nevin, Deb Mailman and Richard Roxburgh; writers such as Tommy Murphy, Rita Kalnejais, Lally Katz and Kate Mulvany; directors including Simon Stone, Benedict Andrews, Wesley Enoch, Rachael Maza and former Belvoir Artistic Director Neil Armfield.

Belvoir's position as one of Australia's most innovative and acclaimed theatre companies has been determined by such landmark productions as *The Diary of a Madman, The Blind Giant is Dancing, Cloudstreet, Measure for Measure, Keating!, Parramatta Girls, Exit the King, The Alchemist, Hamlet, Waiting for Godot, The Sapphires, Who's Afraid of Virginia Woolf?* and *Stuff Happens.*

Belvoir receives government support for its activities from the Federal Government through the Major Performing Arts Board of the Australia Council and the State Government through Arts NSW.

Belvoir Donors

We give our heartfelt thanks to all our donors for their loyal and generous support.

Foundation Donors

Make a significant financial investment in the Belvoir Creative Development Fund.

Neil Armfield AO
Anne Britton
Rob Brookman & Verity Laughton
Andrew & Cathy Cameron
Janet & Trefor Clayton
Anne & Michael Coleman
Hartley & Sharon Cook
Gail Hambly
Anne Harley
Hal & Linda Herron
Louise Herron & Clark Butler
Victoria Holthouse
Peter & Rosemary Ingle
Ian Learmonth & Julia Pincus
Helen Lynch
Frank Macindoe
Macquarie Group Foundation
David Marr
Ann Sherry & Michael Hogan
Victoria Taylor
Mary Vallentine AO
Kim Williams AM &
Catherine Dovey

2011 Chairs Group

Supports the creative development of Indigenous work at Belvoir.

Anonymous (2)
Antoinette Albert
Jillian Broadbent AO
Keith & Leslie Bryant
Jan Chapman & Stephen O'Rourke
Louise Christie
Warren Coleman & Therese Kenyon
Kathleen & Danny Gilbert
Girgensohn Foundation
Marion Heathcote & Brian Burfitt
HLA Management Pty Ltd
Belinda Hutchinson AM
The Jarzabek Family
Cassandra Kelly
Hilary Linstead
Ross McLean & Fiona Beith
John Morris
Cajetan Mula (Honorary Member)
A.O. Redmond
Michael Rose & Jo D'Antonio
Ann Sherry AO
Victoria Taylor

Penny Ward
David & Jen Watson
Dr Candice Bruce & Michael Whitworth
Kim Williams AM
Cathy Yuncken

2011/2012 B Keepers

Income received from B Keepers underpins all of our activities.

B Keepers
Anonymous (5)
A & R Maxwell
Robert & Libby Albert
Gil Appleton
Claire Armstrong & John Sharpe
Berg Family Foundation
Bev & Phil Birnbaum
Max Bonnell
Ellen Borda
Anne Britton
Dr Catherine Brown-Watt
Mary Jo & Lloyd Capps
Brian T. Carey
Elaine Chia
Jane Christensen
Louise Christie
Peter Cudlipp & Barbara Schmidt
Suzanne & Michael Daniel
Chris & Bob Ernst
Jeanne Eve
Peter Fay
Peter Graves
David & Kathryn Groves
Sophie Guest
David Haertsch
Wendy & Andrew Hamlin
Beth Harpley
John Head
Marion Heathcote & Brian Burfitt
Michael & Doris Hobbs
Peter & Jessie Ingle
Rosemary & Adam Ingle
Anita Jacoby
The Jarzabek Family
Avril Jeans
Rosemarie & Kevin Jeffers-Palmer
Margaret Johnston
Rob & Corinne Johnston
Phil Kachoyan
Colleen Kane
Antoinette le Marchant
Jennifer Ledgar & Bob Lim
Stephanie Lee
Atul Lele

Hilary Linstead
Prof. Elizabeth More AM
Dr David Nguyen
D & L Parsonage
Timothy & Eva Pascoe
Richard & Heather Rasker
Greg Roger
Geoffrey Rush
Andrew & Louise Sharpe
Peter and Jan Shuttleworth
Edward Simpson
Chris & Bea Sochan
Victoria Taylor
Judy Thomson
Sue Thomson
Brian Thomson & Budi Hernowibowo
Mary Vallentine AO
Alison Wearn
Judy & Sam Weiss
Paul & Jennifer Winch
Iain & Judy Wyatt

Corporate B Keepers

Constructability Recruitment
Macquarie Group Foundation
Sterling Mail Order

Education Donors

Provide opportunities for young people throughout NSW to access our work.

Anonymous (5)
Ian Barnett
Judy Binns
Jan Burnswoods
Rae de Teliga
Jane Diamond
Priscilla Guest
Julie Hannaford
Siobhan Hannan & James Talbot
Beth Harpley
Dorothy Hoddinott
Susan Hyde
Peter & Rosemary Ingle
Stewart & Jillian Kellie
Robyn Kremer
Margaret Lederman
Zula Nittim
Patricia Novikoff
Judith Olsen
Martine Robins
Peter & Jan Shuttleworth
Chris & Bea Sochan
The Spence Family
Kerry Stubbs
Jane Westbrook
Zee Yusuf

Belvoir Staff

18 Belvoir Street, Surry Hills NSW 2010
Email mail@belvoir.com.au Web www.belvoir.com.au
Administration (02) 9698 3344 Facsimile (02) 9319 3165 Box Office (02) 9699 3444

Artistic Director
Ralph Myers
General Manager
Brenna Hobson

Belvoir Board

Anne Britton
Rob Brookman
Andrew Cameron (Chair)
Peter Carroll
Michael Coleman
Gail Hambly
Brenna Hobson
Frank Macindoe
Ralph Myers

Belvoir St Theatre Board

Trefor Clayton (Chair)
Stuart McCreery
Angela Pearman
Nick Schlieper
Kingsley Slipper

Artistic & Programming

Associate Director – New Projects
Eamon Flack
Associate Producer
Tahni Froudist
Associate Artist
Stefan Gregory
Literary Manager
Anthea Williams
Resident Director
Simon Stone
PlayWriting Australia Resident Playwright
Tommy Murphy
PlayWriting Australia Associate Playwrights
Kit Brookman
Nakkiah Lui
Mei Tsering

Education

Education Manager
Jane May
Education Resources & Regional Access
Cathy Hunt

Administration

Artistic Administrator
John Woodland
Administration Coordinator
Maeve O'Donnell

Finance & Operations

Head of Finance & Operations
Richard Drysdale
Financial Administrator
Ann Brown
Accounts/Payroll Officer
Susan Jack
IT & Operations Manager
Jan S. Goldfeder

Box Office

Box Office Manager
Katinka Van Ingen
Assistant Box Office Managers
Tanya Ginori-Cairns
Alana Hicks

Front of House

Front of House Manager
Ohmeed Ahi
Assistant Front of House Manager
Brooke Louttit

Development

Development Manager
TBC
Partnerships Coordinator
Zoë Hart
Philanthropy Coordinator
Pearl Kermani

Marketing

Marketing Manager
Tina Walsberger
Marketing Coordinator
Marty Jamieson
Publications Coordinator
Gabrielle Bonney
Publicist
Elly Michelle Clough

Production

Production Manager
Chris Mercer
Production Coordinator
Eliza Maunsell
Technical Manager
Len Samperi
Resident Stage Manager
Luke McGettigan
Construction Manager
Govinda Webster
Head Mechanist
Damion Holling
Costume Coordinator
Judy Tanner
Downstairs Technical Supervisor
Jack H. Audas Preston

25 BELVOIR STREET

Edited by Robert Cousins. Foreword by David Marr.

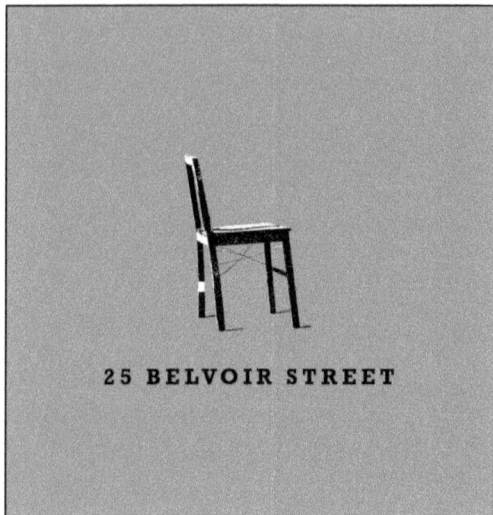

This stunning new book, full of essays, memories and vivid photographs, celebrates a quarter of a century of theatre at Belvoir. Including a collection of essays by Robert Cousins, Ralph Myers, Benedict Andrews, Neil Armfield, Robert McFarlane, Rhoda Roberts, James Waites, Alan John and Rita Kalnejais, *25 Belvoir Street* traces the social and political background from which Belvoir emerged and looks at the way the building itself has found a way into our imaginations.

From its first mercurial decade when it teetered on the edge of oblivion on more than one occasion, through to the appointment of Neil Armfield as Artistic Director, and beyond to a new generation of theatre makers headed by Ralph Myers, this book provides an extraordinary and intimate record of a company that has been described simply as the "heart and soul of Australian theatre".

Creative Development — the lifeblood of theatre

Babyteeth is a new Australian play that has been commissioned and developed through the Belvoir Creative Development Program. We would like to thank our Creative Development Fund donors whose extraordinary generosity enables us to seed and nurture the next generation of Australian theatre. We have now reached over $550,000 of our $1 million target for the fund, which we invest in emerging directors, script development, longer rehearsal periods and works of scale.

Belvoir would like to thank our generous and faithful Creative Development donors for their ongoing support.

Neil Armfield AO
Anne Britton
Rob Brookman & Verity Laughton
Andrew Cameron
Janet & Trefor Clayton
Anne & Michael Coleman
Hartley & Sharon Cook
Gail Hambly
Anne Harley
Hal & Linda Herron
Louise Herron & Clark Butler
Victoria Holthouse
Peter & Rosemary Ingle

Ian Learmonth & Julia Pincus
Helen Lynch
Frank Macindoe
Macquarie Group Foundation
David Marr
Ann Sherry & Michael Hogan
Victoria Taylor
Mary Vallentine AO
Kim Williams AM

If you would like more information about the Belvoir Creative Development Fund, please contact Pearl Kermani on 02 8396 6219 or email pearl@belvoir.com.au

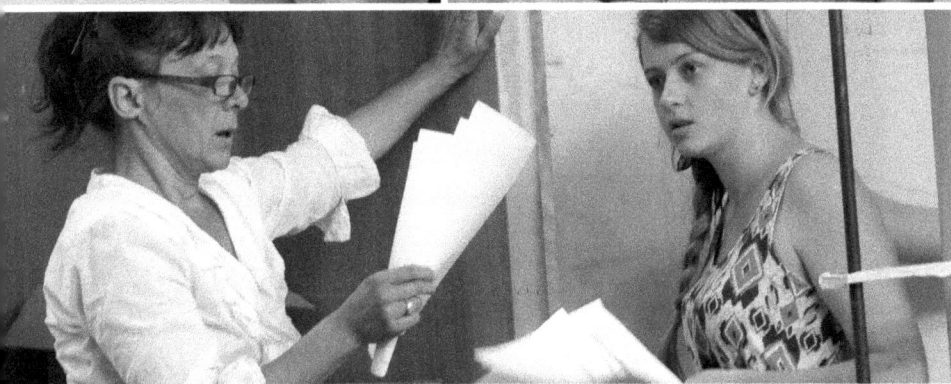

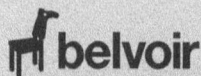

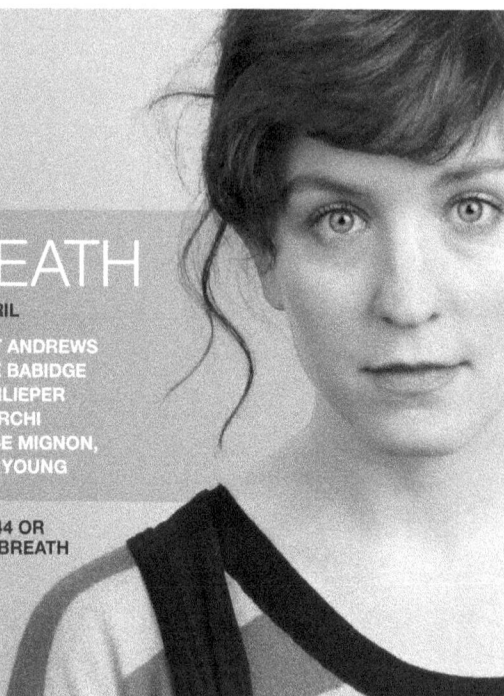

Friendly

Furious

Smitten

Heartbroken

Devious

Overjoyed

At Optus, we know our role in theatre.

OK, so Optus aren't the world's finest thespians. But we do know how to make theatre possible for everyone, through our special collaboration with Belvoir. Our unique 'Charitable Tickets' and 'Unwaged Performance Programs' offer free tickets to those who rarely have the opportunity to enjoy the theatre.

belvoir | 'yes' OPTUS

OPT11094

Helen Buday & Sara West

Set model

Eamon Flack, Eamon Farren & Helen Buday

Belvoir Sponsors

Corporate Partner

'yes' OPTUS

Major Sponsors

AVANTCard

The Sydney Morning Herald
smh.com.au

BAKER & McKENZIE

eye

woolcott research

ERNST & YOUNG
Quality In Everything We Do

Supporters

THE BALNAVES FOUNDATION

Indigenous Theatre at Belvoir
supported by The Balnaves
Foundation

CITY OF SYDNEY

Besen Family Foundation
Coca-Cola Australia Foundation
Enid Irwin Charitable Trust
managed by Perpetual
Events & Stays in the Vines
Gandevia Foundation
The Greatorex Foundation
Media Tree
Teen Spirit Charitable Foundation
managed by Perpetual
Thomas Creative
Vincent Fairfax Family Foundation

Associate Sponsors

PALACE CINEMAS
Share our passion.

Goldman Sachs

REGENTS COURT

Event Sponsors

VINI

bird cow fish

LOTTE SUPREME

James Squire

Al Aseel
RESTAURANT

Cellarmasters

Silver Spoon Caterers

Government Partners

Australian Government

Australia Council
for the Arts

NSW GOVERNMENT | Trade & Investment Arts NSW

For more information on partnership opportunities please contact our
Partnerships Coordinator Zoë Hart on 02 8396 6209 or email zoë@belvoir.com.au

www.ingramcontent.com/pod-product-compliance
Lightning Source LLC
Chambersburg PA
CBHW041931090426
42744CB00017B/2007